Struck Down,
Not Destroyed

Struck Down, Not Destroyed

*Keeping the Faith
as a Vatican Reporter*

Colleen Dulle

IMAGE
NEW YORK

Image
An imprint of the Penguin Random House Christian Publishing Group,
a division of Penguin Random House LLC
1745 Broadway, New York, NY 10019
imagecatholicbooks.com
penguinrandomhouse.com

Library of Congress Cataloging-in-Publication Data
Names: Dulle, Colleen, author.
Title: Struck down, not destroyed / [Colleen Dulle].
Description: New York: Image, an imprint of Random House, a division of
Penguin Random House LLC, [2025] | Includes bibliographical references.
Identifiers: LCCN 2024041050 (print) | LCCN 2024041051 (ebook) |
ISBN 9780593728420 (hardback) | ISBN 9780593728437 (ebook)
Subjects: LCSH: Catholic Church—History—21st century. |
Reporters and reporting—United States. | Journalists—United States.
Classification: LCC BX1390 .D84 2025 (print) | LCC BX1390 (ebook) |
DDC 282.09/05—dc23/eng/20250206
LC record available at https://lccn.loc.gov/2024041050
LC ebook record available at https://lccn.loc.gov/2024041051

Printed in the United States of America on acid-free paper

1st Printing

First Edition

The authorized representative in the EU for product safety and compliance is
Penguin Random House Ireland, Morrison Chambers, 32 Nassau Street,
Dublin D02 YH68, Ireland. https://eu-contact.penguin.ie

For Simon and William

We are afflicted in every way, but not constrained; perplexed, but not driven to despair; persecuted, but not abandoned; struck down, but not destroyed.

—2 Corinthians 4:8–9

Foreword

James Martin, SJ

Lament. It is a word simultaneously used everywhere and rarely understood properly. To lament, at least in the biblical sense, is not just to complain. It is to express grief in a way that seeks understanding, redress, explanation, the reordering of an injustice, and much more. God's Chosen People in the Bible were not afraid of lament, not even when it took the form of criticizing or accusing God. "How long, O God?" begins Psalm 13. Between the book of Lamentations and the Psalms, as many as a third of which are laments, the Bible gives us a wealth of this kind of conversation with God. While no one wants to be put in a place of lament, the religious person knows that it is sometimes necessary.

It is also a practice that struck me time and again while reading an early draft of Colleen Dulle's *Struck Down, Not Destroyed*. Her account of her own work as a conscientious and faithful reporter in the Catholic Church that has been roiled by scandal and stained by sin has more than a hint of the biblical practice of lament running throughout it. Through Colleen's own personal story and the stories of others—not just the bishops, priests, and church figures who play a significant role in her story, but also the victims of sexual abuse, misogyny, and more—she lays out for us a portrait of a current-day Catholic who finds joy in her faith but also increasingly recognizes the injustices and unjust structures that often belie our claim to be the People of God.

This book is a must-read for anyone who wants to understand what young Catholics face today—but also for anyone who wants to answer the question: Why do they stay? Amid a lot of hard stories, the story that runs through the entire book is of a disciple striving to be faithful and to answer a call, a vocation, with integrity and honesty—and with a lot of needed prayer.

I first met Colleen more than seven years ago, when she came to work with us at *America* as a Joseph A. O'Hare Fellow, one of three interns who do a yearlong postgraduate fellowship at the magazine every year while learning the ropes of the journalism business. We ask a lot of our O'Hare fellows (while not quite compensating them with as much rigor!), who work long hours at what are not always the most glamorous tasks. They usually tend to find an area where their skills are best suited and where they can most be of help: writing, editing, researching, audio and video production of our films and podcasts, and more. Colleen was a godsend: She was good at all of them. Smart, energetic, inquisitive, funny, and prayerful: a rare combination.

Fresh off an internship at Catholic News Service when she came to *America,* she had been the editor of her student paper and had freelance writing experience as well. A graduate of Loyola University New Orleans and already a friend to many Jesuits, she also just "got" how a Jesuit ministry works. She understood the church with the wisdom of a Catholic-land veteran, and she wasn't fazed a bit to work with priests and brothers as well as the laypeople who make up the vast majority of our staff these days. She also brought a joy to her work that was infectious, and her frequent laughter and energetic presence brought new life to our team.

We had a (supposed) rule back then with the O'Hare fellows: they couldn't work for us after their year was finished. The idea was that we should force them to leave the nest, to envision their future in new and different ways. Of course, it also means you spend a year with someone, working, praying, playing, and getting to know them in a close personal way, and then you lose them. And you lose them just as they're fully tuned up to do the work of a savvy multimedia journalist!

By my count, we've broken that rule four times in the last six years, unable to pass up the chance to keep valued colleagues in other positions at the magazine. Colleen was the one who prompted us to break that rule, without much regret; we hired her soon after her fellowship ended. We couldn't lose that kind of talent. She's been with us since in a variety of roles and now serves as an associate editor and the cohost of our *Inside the Vatican* podcast; she also continues to write and edit on a regular basis. In fact, our print issue that just went to bed as I was finishing this includes her book review of Mary Ann Glendon's *In the Courts of*

Three Popes and her article on the origins of the Synod on Synodality's "Conversation in the Spirit" method.

Colleen grew up in a church roiled by sex abuse, as readers will see from her accounts of a childhood and educational journey that was steeped in Catholicism. Nevertheless, that first year after we hired her full-time—actually, the first *month* after we hired her full-time—provided some new lows in a miserable story. It was a dismaying and discouraging one for all of us who work in Catholic media. Strike that: a dismaying and discouraging one for *everyone* in the church. Further allegations of abuse and cover-up by priests and church officials from around the world were joined in August of that year by the revelation of repeated sexual abuse of children and vulnerable adults by then-Cardinal Theodore McCarrick.

The former archbishop of Washington, D.C., and a prominent figure in the Catholic Church in the United States and the Vatican for many years, McCarrick was a well-known and revered figure by many Catholics. At *America,* too, at the time, we considered him a friend and colleague; he preached at our 100th Anniversary Mass in 2009 at St. Ignatius Loyola Church in New York. For us as much as anyone, the horrific reports of his criminal behavior came as a shock. Worse, they were unrelenting; it seemed like the stories of abuse by him and others would never end. Those stories make for hard reading, but they make for even harder writing and reporting. At one point we brought in a counselor to talk to the staff about "vicarious trauma," because everyone was a bit shell-shocked. I can't imagine what it was like for someone only twenty-three years of age at the time to be immersed in that maelstrom.

McCarrick's crimes—he was eventually removed from the priesthood and stripped of his cardinal title—were followed in the Catholic news cycle by another startling development in the church. Archbishop Carlo Viganò, the former nuncio to the United States under previous popes, took the opportunity of Pope Francis's visit to Ireland to demand that the pope resign. The pope, Viganò alleged, had known of McCarrick's crimes but had impeded the Vatican's attempts to sanction him and had even covered up his misdeeds. While Viganò's accusations proved unfounded and were followed by year after year of increasingly unhinged claims about Pope Francis, the church, and a supposed worldwide conspiracy to control the world (he's since been excommunicated, which hasn't quite chastened him), the allegation itself came as a shock.

It was almost unprecedented for a bishop of any stripe to demand that a pope resign, but Viganò proved to have powerful allies who wanted nothing more than to rid themselves of a troublesome pope. The secular media took up the story alongside Catholic publications, and once again we found ourselves in the midst of a tornado, bombarded day and night by information not always easily processed or understood. A good spiritual director would tell you to pray your way through such difficulties, but a good spiritual director would also remind you that sometimes even your normal prayer routine isn't enough. Sometimes you have to cry out.

Colleen relates those days in this book with clarity and honesty, reflecting on the struggle it caused within her to trust and believe in the church. When one of her heroes (and mine), L'Arche founder and "living saint" Jean Vanier, was revealed to have been a serial abuser of vulnerable adults for years in his religious community, she writes, it all began to feel like too much. Once again, a figure through whom she found meaning and identity, an icon of Christian discipleship, turned out to be a moral monster. Finding herself brought to tears and struggling to experience the joy she had always taken in Mass and church life, she faced a question I raised earlier: Why do I stay? And where is God in all of this?

Her answer was not to leave, but it was also not to bury her head in the sand. Instead, it was to continue on with her good work and to continue participating in church life, knowing that there was, as we say, "more to the story" than just sin and bad news and unjust structures of deceit. But she does not shy away in this book from the pain, and her accounts of how she dealt with it will strike every reader as courageous and authentic. Imagine telling someone about a retreat on which you found yourself sobbing in church, beseeching God for answers; then imagine how much more vulnerable you would have to be to tell that to an audience of readers who are mostly strangers to you. It takes courage, courage that Colleen shows here in spades.

As her book makes clear, she still sees injustice and deceit present all around, not least in the workings of the Vatican itself, but she shoulders on, "bearing the weight of reality," to quote the martyred Jesuit Ignacio Ellacuria. To do so requires lamentation, a crying out to God in ways that don't always feel "right" to the believer but that are necessary. Remember what the anonymous speaker related in Lamentations 3:13–18?

> He pierced my heart with arrows from his quiver. I became the laughingstock of all my people; they mock me in song all day long. He has filled me with bitter herbs and given me gall to drink. He has broken my teeth with gravel; he has trampled me in the dust. I have been deprived of peace; I have forgotten what prosperity is. So I say, "My splendor is gone and all that I had hoped from the Lord."

Words spoken in pain, vivid images that make clear the cry of the one lamenting: *Where are you, God?* It was the belief of the ancient Israelites—as it is our belief today—that God does not respond to such lament with anger or disdain. Rather, God remains with us even through the pain experienced by the one lamenting. Furthermore, lament is necessary because *without lament, the believer will never heal.* It is no more authentic to the Gospel to live life with relentless positivity than it is in constant negativity. Both are toxic to one's mental health and to one's faith. A genuine lament is one that expresses the truth and cries out in response.

Every reader of this book will see in Colleen Dulle's story her own desire to find healing in her lament, to find a way forward for herself and for the church that is authentic and true. The stories she relates will fascinate readers, but they will also inspire them, I think—inspire them to see not a tale of woe but a tale of integrity and desire by a faithful disciple of Christ. There are so many people I want to give this book to as a gift.

Because she has been working remotely the past few years since Covid-19 changed the way we all work together, and because my own travel requirements mean I'm not in the office every day myself, too often the only time I see Colleen is on a screen during our morning news huddle at *America*. Every time I see her face (sometimes accompanied by her adorable son, William), though, it brings a smile to my face. She's a wonderful colleague and friend. And the more I work with her, the more I am impressed with her energy, her drive, and her professionalism. I would trust Colleen's work on any story about the church—really, any story about anything.

At the time of this writing, Colleen is preparing for a monthlong visit to Vatican City to cover the second session of the Synod on Synodality for *America*. She's been discreetly learning Italian to prepare (she already has French under her belt), and during her work on *Inside the Vatican* with our Vatican correspondent Gerard O'Connell these past few years, she's developed a large network of Vatican contacts and other journalists, so we're expecting great things from her over there. (Actually, I'll be there, too.) She'll be doing what she does best: writing, editing, reporting, and providing our readers and viewers with an honest, informed, charitable take on the news coming from that historic event in that historic place.

Those experiences will hopefully find their way into one of Colleen's future books. There will be many, I think, because this is a superb writer, and a superb person, with much more to say.

Contents

A Hard-won Faith

No Catholic I know has an uncomplicated relationship with the church. Whenever I tell someone I am a Vatican reporter, their first question is always "Are you Catholic?"

Those who were raised in the church often have a deeply held sense of the divine, even while they sometimes harbor doubts that God exists or whether a Catholic understanding of God is the right one. Almost every Catholic struggles to accept certain aspects of the church's teaching, and surveys have shown time and again that most U.S. Catholics don't follow church teaching on a number of issues. The people I speak with often feel alienated by other Catholics for not being "good enough"—for not being the "right kind" of Catholic or not living up to an imagined ideal. Most of all, many Catholics feel deeply scandalized by the church and its leaders because of abuse, corruption, cover-ups, and reluctant apologies. These Catholics understandably question whether or to what degree they can remain in this institution. They are caught in a crisis of conscience: They don't know whether they can stay or whether they can really leave. They question to what extent their relationship with the church affects their relationship with God. Under this seemingly untenable pressure, Catholics have a range of responses, from repudiating the faith completely to joining cloistered monasteries.

As a lifelong Catholic, I've felt all of these things. When acquaintances ask if I'm Catholic after learning about my job, I usually say, "Conflictedly so." But there's another, truer, more complicated, and more vulnerable answer. Among people I trust, I describe my Catholicism as "hard-won."

I know from the experience of having it shaken that my faith is not going anywhere. But to this day, I feel embarrassed to admit that. I am not conflicted about my Catholicism itself but about my connection to an institution whose ugliness threatens to eclipse its beauty.

As a reporter who has focused on the Vatican for several years—hosting a weekly podcast about it, writing and editing articles and analysis pieces, commentating for other news outlets—I have a close-up view of some of the most distressing stories in the Catholic Church. Because of this, and because, for many of my friends, I am the one person they know who still goes to church, they often ask me to explain the stories behind the headlines they've seen about the church and to help them process what these stories can possibly mean for their relationships with Catholicism. I never have definitive answers. The best I've been able to offer is an accounting of my own reporting on the story, my analysis of root causes, and my own honesty about how I've had to grapple with my faith as a result of the story or while covering it.

Through years of these conversations, I've learned that hearing and sharing stories can ease the heartache and facilitate some healing—that grappling with painful truths together is better than doing it alone. I've learned that the community of Catholics who share their pain and grief over the church's scandals often need to be reminded that they are just as much the church, and just as Catholic, as the people who govern the institution. And that feeling conflicted about your religious identity after a scandal is not a sin; it's normal. As former Vatican reporter David Gibson wrote, there is a "constant struggle of conscience required for a Catholic to remain in the church, or for an outsider to join."[1]

It's that requirement and my belief in the value of these conversations that compel me to share this book. It's a bit of a hodgepodge in terms of genre: part reporting and journalistic analysis, part reflection on my spiritual struggles with the church, woven together. In each chapter, I dig into one scandal I've covered, explaining what happened, the reasons behind it, and sharing my own experience of grappling with faith as a consequence. I cover the clerical sexual abuse scandal, women's role in the church, the brewing schism among U.S. Catholics, the financial corruption in the Vatican's saint-making office, the revelations about L'Arche founder Jean Vanier's sex cult, and, in the final chapter, what I make of Pope Francis's ongoing "synod on synodality" reform process.

Most of these are ugly topics, but I think it is important to tell the truth about them and, to the same degree, to tell the truth about my own faith: not just the times it was shaken but the times it found surer footing, when it consoled me in the face of disappointment, grief, and fear. The truth is not in one of those stories or the other but in how they are intertwined.

Sharing these personal stories so widely scares me. As a reporter, I've been trained to keep myself out of the story, which as a reporter, I still try to do. But in my interpersonal conversations, I've found that honesty about my struggles in faith have helped others to feel less alone in theirs and helped us all toward healing. That's why I'm doing this.

WHEN I WAS growing up, I had a sense of religious ecstasy, one that only grew more intense when, in my early teens, I saw a nun praying at my school. The light through the stained-glass windows made a multicolored halo in her gray hair, and as she breathed in, a smile of pure peace and contentment spread across her face. I wanted to experience what she was feeling myself, so I began to pray the way she always told us students to: quieting myself, opening my heart, just sitting with God. Later, a Carmelite brother I was close to would describe this to me as "gazing at God as one lover to another," and although I couldn't have described it that way then, that was how it felt.

I became a little teen mystic, or perhaps a zealous convert, writing melodramatic poetry about God, having dreams in which saints spoke to me. Of course, with time and age, those uninhibited experiences of grace came fewer and farther between. I replaced them with an intellectual fervor—perhaps a predictable path to take, given that Benedict XVI was pope, the Catholic blogosphere was packed with apologetics content, and I was a teenager with a laptop. My friends and I were all beginning to think critically about the religion in which we'd been raised and schooled for our entire lives, and I wanted to understand the rationale behind every teaching. I needed to know what philosophy underpinned the religion in which I'd experienced so much beauty, and I wanted to be able to explain it to friends who were asking the same questions and concluding that Catholicism didn't have much to offer them.

In my quest to understand the church well enough to communicate about it, I had to puzzle through every logical step of whatever teaching I was examining, a monthslong process I would undertake in prayer and writing whenever I had the chance. Oftentimes I ended up reaching the same conclusion as the church, but other times I did not. Either way, conclusions were rarely settled for more than a couple of years, at which point they would be challenged by some experience I had, and I would have to reevaluate, grappling with the teachings and my reality anew.

In this way—at risk of sounding too pious—my search for God and for the truth were always one and the same. It is probably unsurprising that I became a reporter, even less so that I became one who focused on the Vatican. As a teenager I had enjoyed explaining complex church topics in an accessible way that I could only reach through a thorough understanding; as an adult, that meant digging into the endless complexity of the institutional church, mired in history and scandal, the exact things that people want explained.

While digging into the truth of the institutional church didn't shake my faith in God—I think my youthful mysticism was too strong a foundation to crumble—it eroded my certainty in the institution, introducing some cracks that have yet to be filled.

The truth of this institution is complex: it is at the same time a mystical, spiritual community where God dwells, one that does great good in the world, and a broken institution, roiled by scandals that are the fault of its own sinful members. But as with so many complex truths and shameful histories, the only true path to healing is honesty. Too many people undertake the challenge of grappling honestly with that truth alone. In this book, I hope to restore, in a small way, that gift of a spiritual community, struggling together with the truth in order to heal.

Struck Down,
Not Destroyed

CHAPTER I

Human Cries and Divine Silence

The first time I saw St. Peter's Basilica, I felt nothing. It wasn't the reaction I'd thought I would have. I was a lifelong Catholic who'd once seriously considered becoming a nun, and who now reported on the Vatican for a Jesuit magazine. But just a few days before, on a silent retreat, I had been red-faced, tears burning down my cheeks, as I hurled all my anger at God for standing by, apparently unmoved, as tens of thousands of children were sexually abused by Catholic priests over decades.

It was winter 2019. The last six months on the religion beat had been wall-to-wall sex abuse coverage, first[1] with the Pennsylvania Grand Jury Report, which recounted in harrowing detail seventy years of abuse and cover-up. Then the once-beloved Cardinal Theodore McCarrick fell from grace after his serial abuse of minors and seminarians was exposed by a few brave survivors and journalists. And finally, there was Archbishop Carlo Maria Viganò's attempted coup, in which he hijacked the church's legitimate reckoning with abuse and the systems that enabled it, twisting it into an eleven-page manifesto regurgitating previously debunked claims that a "lavender mafia" of gay priests was to blame for the abuse crisis and claiming that Pope Francis himself had covered for McCarrick.

Reporters quickly shot holes through Viganò's argument, pointing out that his own calendar contradicted his timeline of events, not to mention that it was well known that Viganò was angry with Francis for refusing to make him a cardinal. This was the same bishop who, as papal ambassador to the United States, had staged a meeting between the pope and Kim Davis, the Kentucky county clerk who had become a conservative hero for denying marriage licenses to same-sex couples. After Davis's lawyers tried to spin the meeting as a papal endorsement, the Vatican came out with an official statement saying it was only a "brief greeting" and "should not be considered a form of support of her position."[2] The political motivations driving this latest "manifesto" on McCarrick were similarly transparent: the document was published simultaneously by several far-right Catholic publications[3] and its release was timed to the second and final day of Pope Francis's already sensitive visit to Ireland, a country where the church's long-held influence was disappearing after its own reckoning with clerical sexual abuse and other scandals.

It was these nauseating facts that I couldn't escape while on retreat, and that I carried with me to Rome.

Covering this news day in and day out, hearing and working to confirm, as much as possible, the harrowing details of how children were abused, along with discerning the intentions of people, like Viganò, who wanted to use victims' trauma to further their own agendas, was, honestly, excruciating. Those of us journalists who were younger had a particularly hard time; we had mostly been shielded from the abuse crisis during the first wave of revelations in 2002, having been too young to understand. Now, we were having to confront the evil within the church as employees and representatives of the institution. We all believed that for the church to move forward in any credible way, it first had to confront the whole truth. That was a sort of mantra repeated by Catholics throughout what we were already calling the "summer of shame": the church needs to face the truth in order to heal.

But that noble aspiration only carried us so far. I, for one, was compensating for the days of reading through the Grand Jury report and fact-checking Viganò's claims by drinking even more than I already did. (Here, the stereotypes of both hard-drinking Irish Catholics and journalists were true.) In fact, I first read the Viganò letter in the bathroom of some bar in Brooklyn I could never locate again.

I can see now that I was drinking so much more because the way I had usually processed difficult things had been ripped out from under me: whereas I used to find comfort slipping into the Adoration chapel in St. Patrick's Cathedral a block away from work at the end of the day, or relaxing into a pew in the church next door to my apartment to just talk through it all with God, now the place I'd gone for consolation had become the focus of my anger. I remember only feeling comforted at Mass one time during that "summer of shame"—it was a Sunday when the first reading was

"Woe to the shepherds who mislead and scatter the flock of my pasture, says the Lord. . . . You have scattered my sheep and driven them away. You have not cared for them, but I will take care to punish your evil deeds" (Jeremiah 23:1–2).[4] Indeed, I thought. This is exactly what our church leaders have done, and they deserve divine punishment. And then, immediately afterward came the responsorial psalm, "The Lord is my shepherd." While the shepherds of the church continued to anger and disappoint me, the true shepherd, God, was there. I clung desperately to that sliver of hope.

I wasn't the only one struggling. *The Washington Post* op-ed section released a video of its many Catholic editors talking about how the abuse revelations had shaken their faith. In my own circle of friends, several people stopped going to church, and some have not come back. One of my colleagues told me that even his parents couldn't bear to go to church anymore, and so as a family they decided to stay home. When I went home in the evenings, I would hang out with my cousin, a Fordham theology student who lived across the hall, and his friends. Like my colleagues, they were questioning whether they'd made the right call by devoting their lives to an institution that had done such reprehensible things. Everywhere I turned, the feeling was the same—to quote Yeats, "Things fall apart; the center cannot hold."

Although the epicenter of the "summer of shame" was the United States, the Viganò letter, dropped during the pope's trip to Ireland and demanding a response from Rome, ensured that its shock waves were felt everywhere. And

Rome, despite remaining silent for two full years before responding to Viganò's claims, felt the need to take action. Pope Francis announced that he was gathering the heads of all the bishops' conferences throughout the world—national and regional organizations of bishops—along with the heads of the world's orders of nuns, priests, and brothers to come to the Vatican for a euphemistically named summit on "the protection of minors." I and other Vatican reporters called it what it was: the summit on sexual abuse.

The conceit was interesting: Pope Francis would bring the world's bishops into one room and force them to sit and listen to personal testimonies from abuse survivors from six continents, in an effort to debunk finally what some bishops persisted in believing since 2002: that sexual abuse was only an "Anglophone" problem. Every bishop needed to learn that abuse was a global problem and that ignoring it in their dioceses would only do more damage.

Most reporters were skeptical: there was no talk before the summit of using the meeting to impose new rules on the bishops for how to handle abuse, to say nothing of consequences for failing to report it or specific penalties for bishops and priests who abused minors or vulnerable adults or covered up abuse. The expectation across the board was that nothing would change. Nevertheless, the summit was going to be a huge media event; several hundred journalists, myself included, had requested temporary accreditation from the Holy See to cover it.

It just so happened that my trip to Rome for the summit perfectly bridged two other trips I already had scheduled: I would be going from a silent retreat in Montréal directly to Rome for the summit, and then to Israel and Palestine to work as a staff member on one of my magazine's guided Holy Land pilgrimages. My faith was wobbly at best and a source of pain most of the time, and I would be facing it head-on in the retreat (Could I even pray anymore?), then marching directly into the center of all the failures—the source of that pain—and, fresh off the disappointment of nothing changing, I'd have to put on a nice and pious face for the pilgrims who had paid an arm and a leg to visit the holiest sites in Christianity.

I sensed I would emerge from this trip either an atheist or, miraculously, someone with new resolve. If God was going to intervene, now would be a good time.

LEARNING TO YELL AT GOD

My dear friend Sylvester, who is my husband's godfather and both his and my former college professor, had been working at a Jesuit retreat center in Montréal, only his second assignment after being ordained a priest. One of his tasks was to attract younger folks for retreats at the center, which mostly drew older retreatants. I had agreed months before to go on a four-day silent retreat there, in part because I hoped Sylvester could help me with the crisis of faith I had been going through.

Jesuit retreats consist of a series of "spiritual exercises"— basically, guided reflections written by St. Ignatius of

Loyola, the founder of the Society of Jesus, better known as the Jesuits, in the sixteenth century. Many of them include imagining yourself in a passage from scripture, either as one of the characters or as an onlooker, and then having a conversation with God or one of the saints about it. I was, admittedly, out of practice—it had been four or five years since I'd last gone on a retreat and done this kind of prayer.

Sylvester, thankfully, knew what I was dealing with. One of the first readings he gave me to reflect on was the story of Jacob wrestling with an unnamed man all night long. They're evenly matched—it takes all night, after all—and at daybreak, having dislocated Jacob's hip but not defeated him, the man asks Jacob to let him go. It's not clear what Jacob is thinking about this man as they wrestle and wrestle, but it seems to become clear to him at some point that the man is God, or maybe an angel. He says he won't let the man go until the man blesses him, and when he gives Jacob the blessing, he also says that Jacob's name will now be Israel. Israel, in turn, renames the place where they wrestled, to memorialize that it was where he had "seen God face to face . . . and yet [his] life has been spared" (Genesis 32:23–31).[5]

I no longer remember whether, as I prayed with this reading, I imagined myself as Jacob, or an onlooker, or both. But I remember being struck by how long a night is. It's a lot of wrestling, and especially frustrating with an opponent who is no stronger or weaker than you. God, of course, was stronger than Jacob, but he chose to make Jacob wrestle all night, even hurting him, before he would change his name and bless him. God could have changed Jacob's name and blessed him at any time. So to wrestle all night—a gritty, intimate, aggravating struggle—must have been important *in itself.* I had to wrestle with God, with the nastiness I was facing daily in the church, with the nastiness that had started to lodge itself in my chest, if I was going to come out of this transformed. Or with any faith at all.

Sylvester gave me a few other exercises to pray with, which I did, but I couldn't shake the nagging feeling that God and I were going to have to have a talk—or a fight, maybe.

It was February in Canada, and the sun was dropping below the horizon at around five in the evening when I stole into the retreat center chapel—a small, sparse room with plastered walls that stretched up to form an arched ceiling, with two small, abstract stained-glass windows in the wall and a low bench around the perimeter. A red candle flickered next to the tabernacle, a hexagonal gold box suspended in a nook in the wall, containing the consecrated bread of the Eucharist, which is to say, God's presence. "Here we go," I thought.

I'd brought no scripture to pray with. I sat on the corner of the bench nearest the tabernacle and leaned forward, elbows on my knees, chin on my fists, and thought about all that I had held back from bringing to prayer for the better part of a year. I thought about the young man, James,[6] who had been groomed and raped by Cardinal McCarrick—who was so close to his family that he called him "Uncle Ted"—from the time James was eleven years old, whose parents, like the parents of so many kids abused by priests, hadn't believed him when he'd said something. I thought about the ones who had been driven to suicide by their experience. I dug through the muck of all I had read, like the detail from the Pennsylvania Grand Jury report about priests secretly marking kids who were easy to molest by giving them little gold cross necklaces, and I hurled them at God. Most of the time I was silent, but my anger sometimes boiled over.

"What the fuck?!" I demanded aloud.

The silent gold box did not respond.

The last of the light faded out of the room's two windows, and I'd only grown angrier and more tired. I started feeling that, at times, God was responding. He would tell me that my caring mattered. I would hurl back that the parents whose complaints had been stonewalled by the church cared, too. I would demand to know why the hierarchy didn't care. He would tell me that the truth coming out was good, that it would make the institution change. I hurled back that 2002 should have been enough to change it, even as I knew that the vast majority of the abuse happened before the Spotlight investigation was published. God was wearing me down, but we kept fighting. It got darker. Years later, I would hear some shockingly phrased marriage advice from Pope Francis: "It is good when the plates are flying." He meant it was better than letting silent resentment grow. That night, I threw every plate I could at that gold tabernacle.

After a few hours—eight or nine o'clock?—Sylvester appeared in the doorframe. He was surprised to see me, and I was embarrassed to be seen, my face red and splotchy from crying and yelling at God. He gently told me that the Jesuits in formation who lived in the community attached to the retreat center would be coming in shortly to pray night prayer and that I was welcome to join.

I love the night prayer of the liturgy of the hours. It is, arguably, the darkest of the daily prayers, as each day begins with reflections on sunrise and the resurrection and ends with reflections on nighttime, Good Friday, and death. It was my favorite because, in college, I had prayed it nearly every night with friends, including Sylvester, who had taught us all of the Latin chants to sing together. It became a comfort to me, something to wind down my evening before I went to sleep. That night in Montréal, I took it as a sign that it was time to stop—that, like the man told Jacob at daybreak, God wanted me to stop now and rest. Singing my favorite chants with the Jesuits that night—my voice lonely and high amid theirs—I felt like the fight was not over (*there is value in the wrestling itself*) but that God was giving me his blessing, and I could rest, somehow changed.

THE BELLY OF THE BEAST

If my spiritual journey felt incomplete after the retreat in Montréal—yell at God, but then what?—it would remain stunted through my three days in Rome. I would be dashing around the Vatican and the surrounding neighborhoods, interviewing people involved with the abuse summit and those who were part of other Vatican stories I wanted to cover, going to press conferences, and recording podcasts and hosting live videos with my *Inside the Vatican* cohost, Gerard O'Connell. I continued to have the sinking feeling that all of this—the sixteen-hour workdays, the bishops traveling to Rome from around the world—would result in no concrete changes.

Perhaps that was why, after dropping my things at the hotel and walking to the Vatican press office with my audio gear to get my press pass, I stopped in front of St. Peter's Basilica for the first time. I leaned against the black railing that stretches across the open side of Bernini's Colonnade and looked up at the looming façade of the cathedral. *It looks like the pictures, I guess.*

I stayed there for a moment, surprised at my own indifference at finally seeing the place that I spent most of my waking hours thinking about.

Shortly after I'd gotten my press pass and stopped for an espresso with a former colleague from Catholic News Service, where I'd previously worked, Gerry texted me to come over to a gate next to the Colonnade. There, a crowd of Vatican journalists I recognized from Twitter and from their author photos was gathered, waiting, apparently, for a group of clerical sexual-abuse survivors who were rumored to have met the pope.

I no longer remember what quotes the survivors gave us that day, though I do remember holding my phone microphone out to Juan Carlos Cruz, a Chilean abuse survivor who had surprisingly become close with Pope Francis after the pope had called him a liar for saying that Bishop Juan Barros Madrid had, as a priest, personally witnessed notorious predator Father Fernando Karadima sexually abusing him. The pope, it turns out, was friends with Bishop Barros. After a widespread outcry, the pope ordered an investigation, and when he learned he had been wrong, he apologized and invited Juan Carlos and two other survivors of the same priest's abuse to the Vatican. The pope also invited all of the Chilean bishops to the Vatican and demanded their resignations; he accepted Bishop Barros's within weeks—almost immediately, in Vatican terms.

The media scrum that afternoon remains sharp in my memory of the conversations I observed between the more seasoned Vatican reporters: the conversations weren't just chats; they were transactions in a sort of information economy. One would drop a little detail or bit of gossip to see whether the other person knew about it and whether they might add something more. Everyone was dropping little bits of information in hopes of hearing some good gossip that they might confirm with their own sources inside the institution, while still trying to protect what they knew and not giving away any scoops. This was not the kind of reporting I had learned in journalism school, yet I found it strangely enthralling: this was the system I would have to get used to if I were to achieve my dream of becoming a Vatican correspondent.

The next day, I went to a press conference inside the Vatican for the first time. It was in an auditorium-style hall and was set to be about the events unfolding inside the summit meetings. It would end up being another crash course in Vatican reporting.

All anyone was talking about that day was a book that was officially published on the first day of the summit, called in Italian *SODOMA,* that is, *Sodom,* and in English, *In the Closet of the Vatican: Power, Homosexuality, Hypocrisy.* The book was a 576-page tome of juicy gossip about Vatican prelates by French reporter Frédéric Martel, revolving around the central thesis that the more publicly homophobic a prelate was, the more likely it was that he was gay and living a "double life" of hookups and orgies. According to the Vaticanists I chatted with, Martel's thesis was right, but even though he said his book was based on interviews with forty-one cardinals, fifty-two bishops, and forty-five Vatican diplomats, it was going to be easy for the Vatican to dismiss because none of it was ever officially confirmed by the institution, and much of it could be called hearsay.

Martel's book had already been circulated as a PDF among Vatican officials and reporters before its publication; I'd been handed an embarrassingly wasteful printed-out copy a few weeks before because my source didn't want a digital trail of forwarding it to me. (One thing I was learning about Vatican reporting: confidential documents are only secret in that you keep secret the name of the person who gave it to you.) Of the hundred or so reporters at the press conference, plus the Vatican officials on the stage, it seemed safe to assume most had at least paged through it. And while most people knew that homosexuality in the priesthood actually had very little to do with priests sexually abusing children,[7] the book's publication at the start of the conference meant that the Vatican was going to have to answer some questions about it.

I sat behind Gerry and his wife, Elisabetta Piqué, the Italy correspondent for the Argentine newspaper *La Nación*. The auditorium was packed. The panelists gave some information on the summit, and when they opened the floor for questions, Elisabetta asked one of the first.[8] She directed it to Archbishop Charles Scicluna, the Vatican's top abuse investigator, who had been Pope Francis's point man in the Chile investigation.

"I wanted to ask you: Today, [when] this important meeting has opened, there's a book coming out that says that in the church, most members of the [clergy] are homosexual," Elisabetta said. She didn't have to say what book it was; everyone knew. "I wanted to ask you if you've read this book, and if you would like to comment on it."

Before the archbishop could respond, the Vatican spokesman, Alessandro Gisotti, jumped in. "I think the book was being published today, and I think it's quite a long book. Clearly I'll leave the answer to you," he said, nodding toward the archbishop, "but it's . . . a bit complicated to read a book in these days" with the meeting going on.

Before he'd finished his sentence, Scicluna jumped in: "No, I haven't read the book. I haven't seen it."

And like that, it was dismissed.

I won't accuse Scicluna of lying; he is widely seen in the Vatican as a very trustworthy person. But what grated against me was how quickly the book had been dismissed, just like the other reporters said it would be, when it did raise legitimate questions about the culture of secrecy around sexuality in the church's hierarchy. Even if the John Jay College of Criminal Justice's milestone 2004 report had ruled out homosexuality as a cause of clerical sexual abuse, the secrecy around all things sexual in the clergy certainly had enabled some of the cover-up that made the abuse crisis so disastrous.

It's not that I expected this kind of nuance to come out in a quick response at a press conference, but it was especially frustrating to me to see Martel's reporting so easily dismissed by someone whose job was to wrestle with the problem of abuse, at the start of a meeting whose purpose was to wrestle with abuse. All this, just after I'd grasped the importance of wrestling with the church's problems as a key condition of my being Catholic. Surely as an archbishop and investigator, Scicluna had done plenty of that wrestling with abuse and its underlying causes, like the secrecy at the center of Martel's book.

Throughout the summit, I was emailing with a producer from a popular news podcast in the United States about possibly coming on her show to analyze the Vatican summit. She, like most reporters following the story, assumed nothing would come out of it. I tried to keep an open mind, but by the end of the summit, the closest the assembly had come to implementing concrete changes had been when Pope Francis handed out a list of twenty-one proposals[9] outlining how to improve the church's response and prevention of child sexual abuse by clergy. It wasn't clear what he wanted the gathered bishops to do with this list; after all, the assembly didn't have any decision-making power as a group. The best they could do was go back to their dioceses, religious orders, and bishops' conferences and try to implement some of these things. So by the end of the four-day meeting, the proposals remained just that: proposals. The producer nixed the interview; if no concrete change had happened, it wasn't worth covering on her show. There had been some talk about follow-ups from the Vatican coming soon, so I held on to some hope for more concrete change and committed myself to asking incessantly about when the follow-ups might come.

Thankfully, after a month, they did begin rolling out, though the changes seemed small and difficult to explain. Exactly a month after the summit ended, the pope issued a new law for the Vatican city-state requiring Vatican officials to report any sex crimes to the Vatican police. Failure to do so could lead to fines or jail time. (The Vatican police have a jail with about four cells; they have a deal with Italy for inmates to serve out longer sentences in Italian prisons.) The same day, he extended the law to apply to all employees of the Roman Curia, the church's central offices in Rome, and to require new employees to be evaluated on their suitability to interact with minors. The pope also issued guidelines for people working within the Vatican, especially its "pre-seminary," where boys as young as twelve studied. The pre-seminary was facing its own unfolding abuse scandal at the time, which would be tried in Vatican courts; in 2024, after the two priest-defendants were acquitted and the school moved outside Vatican City, one of the acquittals was overturned.

Changes that affected people outside Vatican City (and the embassies that are considered Vatican territory) came in May, just over two months after the meeting concluded. They came in the form of *Vos estis lux Mundi* ("You are the light of the world"), a declaration that made all clergy and vowed religious brothers and sisters mandated reporters of abuse and cover-up. Importantly for adult survivors of abuse, it expanded the categories covered by abuse laws to include "vulnerable adults," a term that provided a lot of room for interpretation but at least gave survivors who had been abused as adults some recourse.

It also set up a new system for having one bishop (the "metropolitan," usually the bishop of the biggest diocese in a region) to investigate another bishop in his region for abuse, to begin within a month of the report being made, requiring investigators to give a report to the Vatican every month of the investigation, and requiring it to be completed within three months. This was meant to prevent cases that were reported from languishing somewhere in the church's internal systems, a problem many survivors and their families had faced, with very little communication from the Vatican, even when cases were eventually decided.

Vos estis also required every diocese to set up a system for reporting abuse cases or cover-ups. It gave them a year to do this, although commentators—myself included—raised questions about whether the Vatican could feasibly enforce this law in its three thousand–ish dioceses around the world. *Vos estis* was temporarily approved for three years, then was expanded to include leaders of lay Catholic groups and made permanent in March 2023.

In December 2019, the pope acquiesced to one of the biggest demands of survivors: that the "pontifical secret" for abuse cases be lifted. This Dan Brown–sounding term referred to the Vatican's highest level of confidentiality—although within the Vatican there is a joke that "a pontifical secret is one you can tell anyone but the pope." The pontifical secret had kept survivors and their families from knowing the details of how their abuse cases had been investigated by the Vatican and how the Vatican had come to a decision. One day, families would just get a notification of a decision out of the blue, if they got one at all, and would not know the rationale behind it. Lifting the secret meant that if international authorities were trying a case that the Vatican had files on, they would now hand them over. According to Gerry's reporting, this decision to lift the secret from abuse cases faced significant internal resistance in the Vatican, perhaps accounting for how long it took to come out.

What I was stuck on, though, was the first proposal from the list Francis had distributed to the bishops at the summit: issuing a handbook that would tell dioceses exactly how to handle abuse cases, step-by-step. The pope had made it clear that the purpose of the summit was to get all of the bishops to understand that sex abuse was an issue in their dioceses; for some of them, implementing the types of systems demanded in *Vos estis* was going to mean building a system from scratch. It would also mean finding resources for such systems, and the dioceses where the bishops insisted that abuse was not an issue were generally poor or otherwise strained for resources because they were in war zones or facing persecution. If the bishops were on the same page about abuse being a problem after the summit, a handbook, I thought, could start to get them on the same page about how to handle it.

The handbook finally came in July 2020. Although it didn't present any new rules, it was the first time the process had been laid out all in one place. It said "abuse" could include a wide range of behaviors including "sexual relations (consensual or non-consensual), physical contact for sexual gratification, exhibitionism, masturbation, the production of pornography, inducement to prostitution, conversations and/or propositions of a sexual nature" committed by a cleric with a minor.

It specified that abuse reports can't be disregarded just because they are made anonymously (one reason reports against McCarrick were originally ignored) and that all reports, even informal ones, that seem at all plausible must be investigated. It required bishops and superiors of religious orders to hand over documents on abuse cases when civil authorities require them, and it stressed that church authorities "must ensure that the alleged victim and his or her family are treated with dignity and respect and must offer them welcome, attentive hearing and support, also through specific services, as well as spiritual, medical and psychological help" and counseled the same for those accused, saying that while bishops have the right to impose restrictions on an alleged abuser's ministry, they should never transfer him to another place.

In 2021, Francis followed all this up with a revision of the Vatican's laws governing punishments for clerical sexual abuse, officially recognizing that adults can be victims of abuse by priests and allowing church authorities to sanction laypeople for sexual abuse. It also criminalized some grooming behaviors for the first time—specifically, those aimed at getting minors or vulnerable adults to engage in pornography—and said a bishop can be removed from office for not reporting sex crimes to church authorities.

There are still a lot of legitimate questions about the church's handling of abuse that remain unanswered. Perhaps the biggest is how the Vatican's understaffed discipline section—a division of its doctrine office—will ever get through its massive backlog of abuse cases. The new laws require reports to be made to the Vatican and investigated on a local level quickly, but abuse cases can still get stuck in the discipline office for years. When the pope appointed his key ally Argentine cardinal (then-archbishop) Victor Manuel Fernández as his new doctrine chief, he specifically told Fernández not to focus on abuse; Vatican sources said this was because further changes were coming to the discipline department. As of this writing, I'm still awaiting any major changes to that department. In the meantime, the disgraceful case of Father Marko Rupnik, a once-beloved Jesuit liturgical artist and high-profile preacher, has played out, raising serious questions about whether he received preferential treatment by the Vatican, the Jesuits, or even Pope Francis after allegedly abusing some twenty women and being temporarily excommunicated for absolving a woman he had had sex with. The Rupnik case could, honestly, have become another chapter in this book, though the full truth has yet to come out. At this moment, Rupnik is a "priest in good standing" in a diocese in Slovenia, after having been kicked out of the Jesuits in 2023.

🍃 🍃 🍃

THE DAY AFTER my tearful night in the chapel in Montréal, I borrowed Sylvester's ice crampons and walked out onto the frozen river behind the retreat center. My face was again red, this time from the cold wind whipping at it. I felt a sense of clarity: The horrifying truths about clerical sexual abuse were going to keep coming out, and it was important that they do. It was important that I not shy away from them, but keep reporting on them, keep trying to reveal the truth. As for how to get through that, which I'd struggled with for months, I now had some direction, too: I had to wrestle and yell at God, and he'd help me to keep going through some kind of grace I had yet to encounter.

"You know my walking-on-water thing, right?" Sylvester asked on my last day in Montréal, referring to a favorite sermon he would give back at Loyola. I remembered. Sylvester liked to use the story of Peter walking to Jesus on the water to talk about how grace works: Peter takes the first step off the boat toward Jesus, and God makes him able to stand on the water. It's only when he doubts that he slips. But that first step is all trust. And that, Sylvester would say, is how grace works: grace is what holds us up, but we have to take the first step of trusting it to catch us, trusting that God will help us do the impossible.

"The last day of a retreat is usually where we do all of the 'God loves you' stuff," Sylvester told me a few hours before I would fly to Rome for the abuse summit. "But we're not doing that," he said, "because you're going into the belly of the beast." Instead of " 'God loves you' stuff," he told me, he was giving me another spiritual exercise to pray with on the plane, on my way into the belly of the beast: Peter walking on water.

🌿 🌿 🌿

I AM STILL LEARNING how to walk on water. I am still here, still reporting on each of these developments, still waiting impatiently for more progress. I am angry about it often. Sometimes I yell at God about it. Sometimes I avoid talking to God at all. Sometimes I step off the boat confidently, trusting that my work is, in some way, making a difference. Oftentimes I don't.

I've found that the hardest part of covering sex abuse is not becoming numb to it. Sometimes that mechanical, crisis-response part of my brain takes over—which is good for writing the news—but the real difficulty is letting myself think about what is happening outside of that specific mindset. When I do that, it opens up a flood of pain, just like it did in that bare-bones chapel in Montréal. I can't tell you I have any answer for it. The wrestling is my best answer.

CHAPTER 2

Women in Leadership

"Girls can't be priests." That is the first, and sometimes the only, time that many young women are told they cannot do something simply because of their sex. Many of my friends who were raised Catholic had this exact experience, and it led several of them either to conclude that Catholicism had nothing to offer them or to study theology and become experts at it in order to prove that they had the same, if not greater, abilities as the seminarians in their classes.

I'm embarrassed to admit that my own awakening to the significance of disparate gender roles in the church didn't come until much later. I was in college, working at the diocesan newspaper in St. Louis. It is a rather traditionalist diocese—my childhood bishop there had been Cardinal Raymond Burke, a leading voice in U.S. Catholic traditionalism and now in the American resistance against Pope Francis. Although Burke was assigned elsewhere in 2008, by the time I returned in 2015 he still had many fans in St. Louis who were interested in carrying forward his legacy. When I worked at the diocesan paper, I struggled with its conservative bent. One colleague noticed this and handed me a printout of an *America* magazine article by Nathan Schneider titled, "The Choreography in Rome." Schneider details attending a Mass and Corpus Christi procession in Rome, where the cardinals, bishops, dignitaries, and priests were seated at the front of St. John Lateran Church, followed by groups of nuns, and then, at the back, everyone else. When the Eucharistic procession through the streets began, "The sea of nuns began surging into a river behind it, with none of the careful pacing and leisure that had been allotted the clerical dignitaries, for in the nuns' case it was clear that the Sacrament would not be waiting around for them." He continues:

> At St. John Lateran there were probably hundreds of men closer to Francis than the closest woman, and given the courtly origins of the choreography, this is a meaningful distance. That distance is distance from power, from voice. This is not complementarity, it is hierarchy. I'm sorry: It is patriarchy. And the church that I love tolerates it, persists in it, insists on it—as if it is of a piece with the beauty of the costumes and the music and the gospel. Peter hid from the cross while Mary stayed, yet his heirs are blocking the view of hers.[1]

It was my first time realizing what had been so obvious to others: that there is a very clear class system in the Catholic Church, and that although, as Schneider writes, "the altar girls and the fierce women in the front pews help to offset the effects" at most parish Masses in the United States, the hierarchy's gradation by ordination status and gender plays out in striking detail in such ceremonies in Rome, at the center of the global church.

I remember reading the article over and over, keeping it on my desk and picking it up on the days when the conservatism of the chancery was getting to me—like when the *Obergefell v. Hodges* Supreme Court decision came down legalizing gay marriage, and the office's somber mood stood in stark contrast with the absolute joy that permeated my Twitter feed that day. Nathan's article was the first time I'd seen someone write honestly and critically about the gender disparity in the church, and it made me feel that maybe there was a place where such discussions could be had freely.

Years later, covering the Vatican's 2018 Synod on Young People, the Faith and Vocational Discernment—a big meeting of the world's bishops to discuss what young people needed from the church—for *America,* where I had begun hosting a weekly Vatican podcast, I learned that the limits on women's decision-making power in the church were not exclusively a matter of ordination. Going into the 2018 synod, participants and reporters raised questions about whether women would be able to vote on the synod's recommendations to the pope. Each time there is a synod, a document of proposals is voted on, paragraph by paragraph, based on the synod body's discussions. The synod then passes on those proposals to the pope, who usually uses it to draft an official teaching document on whatever the synod was discussing. The synod makes proposals, while the pope decides which, if any, he will codify into church teaching.

The question about voting came up because at the previous synod, in 2015, a non-ordained religious brother of the Little Brothers of Jesus, Hervé Janson, had been allowed to vote. Up to then, the only people who could vote were the bishops and the heads of men's religious orders participating in the synod, who were all ordained priests. (Women who headed their religious orders never had a vote; they were only allowed to participate as "auditors.") Brother Janson was an exception—the head of his order, but a brother, not a priest. When he was permitted to vote, which some have chalked up to an accidental oversight, it meant that the ability to vote was no longer limited to the ordained—it was limited to men, regardless of ordination status.

Although the Janson case sparked a worldwide movement advocating for women to be given a vote in the synod, which Janson himself and other heads of male religious orders backed, along with religious sisters and laywomen, women weren't allowed to vote in the 2018 or 2019 synods. Meanwhile, the lay brothers' right to vote was affirmed for both synods. In other words: the Vatican repeatedly approved lay men's right to vote while denying that right to women who held the same ecclesial status.

Up until I covered this story, I had always been willing to accept the gender disparities in the church to a certain extent because I trusted the church's teaching on the male-only priesthood: I thought all the disparities I saw could be chalked up to women not being ordained, and although I was never completely convinced by the arguments for a male-only priesthood, I was willing to accept the teaching anyway as an act of faith, trusting that God must be at work through it in a way I did not understand. In the case of women being denied a vote while lay men were allowed one, though, there was no such explanation possible; no matter how much faith or humility I tried to muster, it remained eminently clear that this double standard was wrong and needed to change.

WOMEN IN THE VATICAN

It started to seem possible in 2020—even likely—that Sr. Nathalie Becquart, a French Xavière sister who played a key role in 2018's Synod on Young People, would be the first woman to vote in a synod when Pope Francis named her one of two undersecretaries (the number-three role) in the Vatican's then-Secretariat of the Synod of Bishops, the body that hosts these meetings. Ordinarily, the people in her office—previously all ordained men—were given a vote at the meetings they hosted. Three years after her appointment, it was still unclear whether she would have the right to vote in the "Synod on Synodality" Roman meetings in 2023 and 2024. It was clear, though, that Pope Francis no longer imagined Sr. Becquart's office to be solely concerned with bishops. In his 2022 reform of the central offices of the Vatican, he knocked the bishops out of the office's title, changing it from the "Secretariat of the Synod of Bishops" to the "Secretariat of the Synod," a change Sr. Becquart told me she believed was significant.

I believe that putting women in positions of leadership in the Roman Curia (the Vatican's governing body) is an important step toward co-responsibility, that is, sharing responsibility for church decision-making between men and women. But those women's stories cannot be appreciated without first considering the women at the bottom of the Vatican's ladder of power, the ones who rarely make the news: the nuns who are assigned to cook and clean the homes of bishops and cardinals in Vatican City and in Rome.

In February 2018, an exposé revealed that religious sisters, often living far from their home countries, were now working domestic jobs in church officials' houses or apartments, and that since many did not have registered employment contracts, they were paid "little or not at all." The report came from an unlikely source: it was published by *Women Church World,* a glossy insert that is included once per month in the Vatican's daily newspaper, *L'Osservatore Romano,* which essentially functions as a public relations publication for the Vatican.[2] The article's author, French journalist Marie-Lucile Kubacki, detailed how the nuns' precarious financial situation—and, in some cases, their equally precarious immigration statuses—made them dependent on their employers and thus more vulnerable to exploitation. One African sister who wished to remain anonymous explained that there were sometimes complex financial situations at play: for example, a woman might join a religious order, and the religious order may take on some of the responsibility for providing for her family. In that case, she may fear that speaking up against abuse could risk her family's security. "These sisters feel indebted," the African sister said. "They feel bound and so they keep quiet."

The labor exposé caught the attention of the international press; a report on it appeared on the front page of *The New York Times* on March 1, 2018. Within the Vatican, *Women Church World* began to receive more, and not necessarily positive, attention—it resulted in increased scrutiny and control, Lucetta Scaraffia, the feminist historian who founded the magazine and served as its first editor in chief, later told me and other journalists.

But the nuns' whole story had not yet been told. As 2018's "summer of shame" unfolded in the Catholic Church, bringing revelations of decades of abuse of children and vulnerable adults by clergy, including the abuse of seminarians and priests by a soon-to-be-removed top cardinal, Theodore McCarrick, the #MeToo movement continued to gain traction around the world. With sexual abuse victims feeling more empowered to speak out, reports in France, Italy, and Chile detailed how women had been abused by priests and other men who were members of religious orders.[3] The reporters at *Women Church World,* meanwhile, were gathering their own information on how nuns were being sexually abused by priests and brothers, who had at times even paid for these women to get abortions. Lucetta told me that a top Vatican cardinal had told her to back off from reporting the story. On February 1, 2019, she published it.[4]

Three weeks later, Lucetta and I sat in her living room in Rome, a bright, high-ceilinged parlor lined with packed bookcases. Vertical bookshelves squeezed into every corner gave the illusion of precariously high stacks of volumes towering over their petite owner. I had scheduled the interview before Lucetta's bombshell article had been published, hoping to ask her about her perception of women's role in the Vatican. Now, her own role was headline news.

Lucetta drew a parallel between her magazine's staff and the women whose abuse she had reported on. In both cases, she said, the women had been overlooked, which had given them a certain freedom to speak out. "In the church up to now, it has been very easy for a woman to live autonomously because the priest does not see her. The priests don't think the women are anything. And that's a freedom for the women in a sense," she told me.[5] "It's the same story with *Women Church World,* our magazine, where we have had a lot of liberty from *L'Osservatore Romano.* . . . The magazine wasn't anything. It wasn't important. And so we have had a lot of freedom."

That freedom, Lucetta said, was limited as soon as the women caught the attention of their superiors. While Pope Francis responded to Lucetta's report by publicly acknowledging for the first time the problem of priests abusing nuns and saying it must stop,[6] Lucetta suspected that the scrutiny she'd been facing ever since the 2018 labor report would now reach a fever pitch. It did, and on March 26, 2019,

Lucetta and the entire editorial board of *Women Church World* resigned in protest.

Lucetta had done her work and exposed the story, but it had consequences. She told the Associated Press—although no one in the Vatican would confirm this—that the new editor of *L'Osservatore Romano,* Andrea Monda, had tried to get her fired when he heard about her reporting. After she presented him with a list of groups that would pull their subscriptions from the newspaper if she were fired, she said, he relented, but "indirect attempts to delegitimize us" began.[7] Monda denied this claim.

That same month, the #NunsToo movement, as it came to be called, continued with more damning stories: a French documentary released in March 2019 detailed alleged sexual abuse of nuns by the famous theologian priest Marie-Dominique Philippe, OP, and his brother, Thomas Philippe, a cofounder of the L'Arche community for developmentally disabled people. (For more on the allegations against the L'Arche founders, see Chapter 4 of this book.) The #NunsToo reports, though, were not coming from inside the Vatican the way *Women Church World*'s reporting had. And although the new staff of the magazine has been more outspoken on women's issues than I initially expected after Lucetta's departure—for example, they denounced clericalism in January 2020—and although there have been significant efforts and reforms in church law to prevent the abuse of minors and vulnerable adults, I'm left wondering who, if anyone, is standing up for the nuns who are in vulnerable positions in the Vatican now.

OPENING DOORS

Hope for women's inclusion and for our voices to be heard is more evident at the higher, more public levels of the Vatican. Pope Francis has accelerated the rate at which women are being appointed to high-ranking leadership positions in the Vatican.

A brief clarification of terms would be helpful here before I dive into the numbers. Vatican governance is split into two separate parts: the Roman Curia and the governatorate (or government) of the Vatican city-state. The Curia handles the "churchy" matters, like evangelization, doctrine, charity, the sacraments, saints' causes, discipline, and so on. The governatorate, on the other hand, handles anything relating to the day-to-day running of the Vatican city-state: the Vatican Museums (a key moneymaker for the Vatican, which are headed by a woman, Barbara Jatta), the Vatican's postal service, its police force, its health and hygiene services, and so on. In November 2021, Pope Francis appointed Sr. Raffaella Petrini to the number-two position in the governatorate, another first for a woman.

On the Curia side—the "churchy" offices—each dicastery (Vaticanese for "office" or "department") is usually led by a prefect, a secretary, and a couple of undersecretaries. When I speak about women being appointed to top leadership positions in these offices, I mean that they have been appointed secretaries or undersecretaries or their equivalents in the handful of offices that are structured differently. We have yet to see a female prefect, although Pope Francis's

2022 reform of the Roman Curia made it possible for women to become prefects in the future.

These top three positions used to be completely off-limits to women; this only began to change shortly after Vatican II, when in 1967 Pope John Paul II appointed Rosemary Goldie as an undersecretary in the Pontifical Council for the Laity. Since then, the number has very slowly increased. In 2009, under Pope Benedict XVI, only three women held top positions; in 2019, under Pope Francis, the number was eight out of eighty to one hundred such roles before a few women left their jobs during the coronavirus pandemic.[8] At the time of this writing, the top woman in the Roman Curia was Sr. Alessandra Smerilli, an Italian economist and nun serving as secretary of the Vatican's Dicastery for Promoting Integral Human Development, a bit of an all-purpose office handling the Vatican's humanitarian work. Another of the top women in the Curia was Sr. Nathalie Becquart, the aforementioned French Xavière nun who was the first woman to be given a top position in the Synod of Bishops.

Likewise, the pope has appointed women for the first time to the Vatican's Dicastery for Bishops, which is the body that selects bishops. Sr. Raffaella Petrini, the top woman in the Vatican City governatorate, was appointed to serve on this body, as was María Lía Zervino, a consecrated laywoman who wrote a fiery open letter to Pope Francis in 2021 asking for greater inclusion of women in top Vatican offices.[9] These appointments, which place women in vital positions formerly reserved for bishops, or in which they are even involved in selecting bishops, would have been un-imaginable only a few years ago. Indeed, not so long ago, priests were automatically made bishops because they were appointed to some of these positions, such that these appointments were a mechanism for advancement for men while women were barred from them.

I would echo Sr. Nathalie Becquart's famous comment on her appointment: "The patriarchal mindset is changing." But with women's inclusion in top leadership positions in the Curia peaking at women holding 10 percent of those positions at best, there is an agonizingly long way to go. Moreover, there is no consensus on where the church should be headed. Gender parity in these leadership roles seems a reasonable goal, but it only became a possibility in 2022 when Pope Francis lifted the ordination requirements for many top curial roles. The Vatican has yet to define exactly which roles still require ordination.

The question of ordination requirements is only one expression of a cultural reality that has upheld the Vatican's "stained-glass ceiling." The culture of the Vatican looks with suspicion on anyone who appears to seek power—and women advocating for greater participation in the church's teaching authority are all too often dismissed as simply being hungry for power.

Power, in the Vatican, is not something to be striven for. In fact, there is a strong taboo against ambition of any sort, for both men and women, though perhaps women are pun-ished more for it. There are, of course, plenty of examples of people jockeying for power, as happened while John Paul II's health declined, for example, but in general, anyone striving for power usually tries not to make it obvious. This taboo is solidified in the structure of how Vatican appointments are made: While in other organizations, there are opportunities for career advancement—and even expectations that one would be promoted after a certain number of years of proven work—there is no structure for putting oneself forward for a promotion to a top role. All of those appointments are made personally by the pope, usually from a short list compiled by his relevant advisers, and it is unimaginable that someone, especially a layperson, would, or even could, ask the pope for such an appointment.

Furthermore, when someone is appointed to a high-ranking position in the Vatican, they generally describe their new role in terms of service to the church, whereas in other professional spheres it is not abnormal to hear someone from a historically marginalized background speak about representing that background in a visible position of power. I don't think this is simply a matter of the Vatican being inherently conservative or lagging behind U.S. culture; rather, ambivalence toward ambition comes from a deeply rooted Christian belief in servant leadership. This isn't corporate jargon: the central claim of the Christian faith is that God chose to be born a poor human and to be put to death as a criminal in Jesus, and that God's humility is something we should emulate.

This culture determines how the question of women's place in the church is framed. It means that discussions of "women's empowerment" are scant in the Vatican, and that creating any measurable equity goals, like gender parity in top roles, simply does not happen. Instead, any goal aimed at women's inclusion is usually framed in more abstract terms like "giving women a seat at the table" and "ensuring women's voices are heard."

Yet it is not clear whether the women's voices are free to be critical. Lucetta Scaraffia and other self-identified feminists have criticized the Vatican for only raising "yes women" through the ranks who will not challenge their male colleagues or bosses. (And, she adds, those "yes women" have never risen past the number-two jobs in their offices. Number one, to this day, is for men only, even lay men.) She told me that, since her departure, "the situation of women in the Vatican today seems to me to have worsened. There is no longer any free voice, in exchange for a few places in medium-high positions without the possibility of changing anything or making a critical voice heard."[10]

Lucetta has argued that not only should women be made members of the pope's council of cardinal advisers (sometimes called his "cabinet," to borrow a political term) but that women could also be made cardinals with a small change to church law, without having to change the church's policy against ordaining women as priests.

I have a slightly more hopeful view of the voice of women in the Vatican today than Lucetta does: In my seven years covering the Vatican at *America,* I have seen more vocal women appointed and given a chance to speak about the shortcomings they see in church leadership. For example, Sr. Nathalie Becquart speaking about the patriarchy at a

Vatican press conference would have been unheard of in the recent past. And the women who are invited to speak at official Vatican events I've covered have even been critical of the bishops to their faces. At the Vatican's 2019 summit on preventing sexual abuse, Sr. Veronica Openibo, a Nigerian nun who had worked in sex education and counseling for nine years in her home country, delivered a powerful speech to the world's bishops urging them to take action on abuse, dismantling many of the arguments that church leaders had made over the years against punitive measures like removing abusers from the priesthood or publishing the names of those credibly accused.

Longtime Vatican correspondent Valentina Alazraki, who reports for the Mexican TV station Televisa, likewise was invited to address the bishops at the summit, and she pulled no punches, speaking first as a mother and then as a journalist:

> For a mother there are no first- or second-class children; there are stronger children and more vulnerable ones. Nor are there first- and second-class children for the church. Her seemingly more important children, as are you, bishops and cardinals (I dare not say the pope), are no more so than any other boy, girl or young person who has experienced the tragedy of being the victim of abuse by a priest. . . .
>
> You may be certain that for journalists, mothers, families and the entire society, the abuse of minors is one of the main causes of anguish. The abuse of minors, the

devastation of their lives, of their families' lives, worry us. We believe such abuse is one of the most reprehensible crimes.

Ask yourselves: are you enemies, as determined as we are, of those who commit abuse or who cover them up?

We have decided which side to be on. Have you done so truly, or in word alone?

If you are against those who commit or cover up abuse, then we are on the same side. We can be allies, not enemies. We will help you to find the rotten apples and to overcome resistance in order to separate them from the healthy ones.

But if you do not decide in a radical way to be on the side of the children, mothers, families, civil society, you are right to be afraid of us, because we journalists, who seek the common good, will be your worst enemies.[11]

Although not Vatican officials, the speeches by Sr. Openibo and Ms. Alazraki show an openness on the part of the Vatican not only to give women who are critical of the church's response to sexual abuse a platform but, more important, to put them in a position where bishops are forced to listen to them.

That openness has been hard-won—and has not always translated to Vatican officials welcoming women among their ranks. Pope Francis said he had to "fight" resistance from other Curia officials when naming Paloma García Ovejero as the first woman in the role of deputy director of the Holy See Press Office, an office where most employees were women, in 2016.[12] She quietly resigned with the office's director, Greg Burke, on New Year's Eve in 2018, a notoriously difficult time for the communications office.

◌   ◌   ◌

I WOULD BE REMISS not to mention one last, deeply engrained source of resistance to women taking on leadership roles: clericalism.

Clericalism is, put simply, the belief that priests are superior to laypeople. To a large extent, Vatican II chipped away at this vision of priests as superior by acknowledging laypeople's central role in the church's evangelizing mission. Yet this clericalism has not been totally expunged: In most parishes, the priest has final say over all decisions—sacramental, financial, and so on. Even in simple matters, "Go ask Father" is a constant refrain. Part of why this idea persists is the misapplication of the church's teaching that priests are "ontologically changed" when they are ordained—a clunky term that essentially means the priest undergoes a real and irreversible spiritual change in order to carry out his ministry. This idea came to be understood in practice, even if never officially, to mean that the vocation of priests is superior to the vocation of the laity. The priest came to be seen as an unimpeachable authority figure who is, on some fundamental, spiritual level, better than the non-priests.

It is hard not to see clericalism in a lot of the resistance to women, and even lay men, taking on Vatican roles. Clericalism is also often a precondition for abuses of clerical power, as in the case of the bishops who exploited nuns for labor or sex. The abuses and resistance are never solely attributable to clericalism, but it is a current that strengthens the other factors at work: sexism, for example, or secrecy, or pride, or a desire for control. Whatever the motive, clericalism provides opportunity to act badly, and it emboldens clergy to act in ways they might not otherwise.

Because the church was for so long run by an all-cleric hierarchy, some of the Vatican's structures and practices have yet to be updated to allow for laypeople, including women, to take on high-ranking Vatican positions. The introduction of lay, and especially female, leadership has therefore created a complex dynamic.

I witnessed this dynamic up close when my good friend Molly Burhans, a global leader in geographic information systems (GIS), received an offer from the Vatican to establish the Vatican Cartography Institute, a brand-new Vatican office that would become the first to have been founded and headed by a woman. Molly is a deeply committed Catholic and environmentalist—she was part of a group of "eco-punks" in her hometown of Buffalo, New York, building green projects like a vertical garden without permission in Buffalo's abandoned industrial buildings. She converted to Catholicism while studying GIS and began living an ascetic lifestyle, considered becoming a nun, and founded her non-profit, GoodLands, on a shoestring budget, with the goal of mapping the Catholic Church's extensive landholdings and helping to use them for environmental and social justice purposes. She became the first person to create a unified digital global map of the Catholic Church, and she's been recognized and given awards by the United Nations, the Sierra Club, and National Geographic, among many others.

Molly is, in short, impressive as hell, and even more impressive when you see the incredible simplicity she lives in—I've seen her through tiny apartments, crashing with nuns, saving money by eating canned beans every day, all while she could easily be making in the high six figures with her GIS knowledge and connections. But when the Vatican offered her the Cartography Institute, their proposal included no budget for operations, and her salary would be the same as what cardinals receive: around $30,000 to $40,000 per year. Even for an ascetic like Molly, it wouldn't be enough money for her to afford to live alone in Rome. It is only manageable for cardinals because they receive exclusive benefits, like Vatican-provided or at least partially subsidized apartments, which are not available to their lay colleagues. (Lucetta Scaraffia, by the way, never received a paycheck for her seven years of work on *Women Church World*.)

Molly sent the Vatican a detailed counterproposal for an institute with a million-dollar annual budget, still small by GIS industry standards, but after two years the Vatican still had not responded. Eventually, at the end of 2021, after a visit to Rome in which the Vatican officials she'd previously worked with refused to meet with her, she decided to move on and accepted work with secular clients.

It wasn't an easy decision, but having seen Molly go through so much back-and-forth with Vatican officials followed by months on end of radio silence from them, it was clear she made the right call. She's still living simply, and, despite the new work, I know she still has hope that the institute could come about in some form. Despite that hope, which I share, I can't help but be frustrated and angry on her behalf: because the Vatican lacked the structures to support a laywoman who is not a member of a religious order as head of a department, even one who was willing to make financial sacrifices to take the job, they not only lost out on the contributions of the world's foremost expert in Catholic landholdings but also ended up discouraging and wearing out one of the most energetic and faithful Catholic women I know.

Until the Vatican can put in place the structures to support lay employees, only women who are members of religious orders or those who are already independently wealthy will be able to accept positions. One baby step on this front was made in June 2022, after the pope removed the ordination requirement for top Vatican positions: a new Directorate for Human Resources was established as part of the Vatican's Secretariat for the Economy, which is meant to provide ongoing professional development (which has been totally absent in the Vatican before now), plus a performance-based compensation system and an effort to break down the silos that keep various departments from working together well, a commonly recurring problem.[13] In 2024, however, the Association of Vatican Lay Workers (essentially the union for lay employees) stated that the concerns it brought to the HR office "have not been received, and even ignored."[14]

WOMEN'S ORDINATION

Considering all of these problems, some are tempted to see ordaining women as a cure-all. I don't think the answer is so simple.

First, let's make clear what we're talking about. There are two kinds of women's ordination that are being debated at the same time right now: ordination to the priesthood and ordination to the diaconate. The debate on the diaconate generally follows these lines: There is a historical precedent for women serving as deacons in the early church, but exactly what their role was is debated. Some argue that deaconesses only existed to minister to women who, for privacy or modesty reasons, couldn't be ministered to by male deacons. Others think that deaconesses' role went beyond that. Another line of argument focuses less on the history of the women's diaconate and more on where the church is now in terms of deacons. Around the year 500, the practice of ordaining permanent deacons—men who would stay deacons rather than it being one step on the way to priesthood— began to decline, and it wasn't brought back until Vatican II in the 1960s. Some use this revival of the permanent diaconate as a starting point and ask whether women can be made deacons according to that model, since they would remain deacons and not become priests. This perspective also focuses on the ways that having more deacons could help in places where there are fewer priests, like in the Amazon rainforest, where communities regularly go more than a year without a visit from a priest, and where an estimated two-thirds of Catholic communities are led by women catechists.

As for ordaining women to the priesthood, I believe the church has only recently achieved a degree of willingness to discuss this topic. In his 1994 document Ordinatio Sacerdotalis ("Priestly Ordination"), Pope John Paul II declared "that the church has no authority whatsoever to confer priestly ordination on women and that this judgment is to be definitively held by all the church's faithful," effectively shutting down discussion of it. In 2008, under Pope Benedict XVI, the Vatican doubled down, declaring that any woman who attempts to be ordained a priest and any bishop who attempts to ordain a woman will be automatically excommunicated. Although Pope Francis has echoed John Paul's declaration, saying early in his pontificate, "That is closed, that door," he allowed for discussions of women's ordination in church-hosted listening sessions as part of the global listening phase of his Synod on Synodality, and even approved a mention of it in the synod's first global report in October 2022, with the report noting that there was a wide variety of opinions on the matter.

This is an important step because it acknowledges that despite John Paul II's order that "this judgment is to be definitively held by all the church's faithful," there is not actually agreement among the Catholic faithful about women's ordination, and church authorities must be willing to examine why rather than shutting down discussion. If the church is truly at the service of an objective truth revealed by the Holy Spirit that says only men can be priests, it will not be afraid of discussion or argument on the topic by Catholics who are dedicated to seeking the truth. In a post–Vatican II church that recognizes the laity as the People of God, through whom God speaks and works in the world, and in a church whose lay theologians serve in top theological bodies like the International Theological Commission and are often better educated than clergy members, clerics at the top of the church hierarchy have no reason to distrust lay participation in these discussions, which are intended to discover, or rediscover, the truth.

Without minimizing the significance of the question of women's ordination, either to the permanent diaconate or to the priesthood or both, it remains the case that the church already has difficulty with women in lay ministry, as Pope Francis has learned when facing resistance to his appointments of women. It is clear that frustration about the ordination of women is really an expression of despair about the role of women in the church generally: if clerics cannot learn to minister alongside women as true partners in the church's work, then of course people will conclude that the problem will only be solved when the church ordains women. Those in the church who wish to uphold traditional teaching on a male-only priesthood therefore have an added incentive to address, seriously and without reservation, the role of laywomen. The theological truth at the heart of the ordination question cannot be isolated from the theological truth that God has called all of the People of God, including and perhaps especially women, to carry out the church's ministry, including its teaching and preaching. I believe it is because the church has failed in its practice to embrace this latter truth that its teaching regarding the former is now in doubt. Or, to say it differently, perhaps the question of women's ordination can only be answered truly, and the answer received by the church's members fully, when the church repents of its failure to embrace and empower women in lay ministry.

FOLLOWING MARY MAGDALENE

Directly after a few whirlwind days of late nights and early mornings covering the Vatican's sexual abuse summit in February 2019, I boarded an Alitalia flight to Tel Aviv, where the next day I would join a group of *America* readers and a few of my co-workers for a pilgrimage through the Holy Land: three days in Galilee, one traveling through the West Bank, and another three days in and near Jerusalem. I was exhausted, having had no time for reflection except a few stolen moments that morning before my flight. I'd gone to St. Peter's Basilica when it opened at six a.m., mainly so that I could say that as the host of a podcast called *Inside the Vatican,* I had actually been inside the Vatican at least once.

When I got inside, my primary feeling was, once again,

ambivalence. I think the only adjective I could muster in that moment, dwarfed by the cathedral's imposing architecture, was "big." I sat in one of the few pews near the front of the church and prayed for the friends I'd promised to pray for, but when it came time for me just to sit with God, I didn't hear much. I remember walking the long way across the marble floors to the door with the clear thought: "I think I'm more of a Galilee Catholic than a Rome Catholic"— a humorously decisive thought for someone who had only just visited Rome for the first time and had never seen Galilee. But I had an inkling that the mustard-bush-covered shores of the Sea of Galilee where Jesus had walked would make me feel more connected to him than the gigantic, cold stone structures and statues of the Vatican could. In Rome, I was continually struck by the dissonance between the hideousness of abuse cover-up and the ornate, frescoed rooms in which such decisions had been made. I could see the surroundings as impressive but not beautiful.

When I reached Galilee, the natural surroundings were indeed beautiful, but time to reflect remained elusive. Despite the retreat organizers' best efforts to make the pilgrimage more of a slow-paced traveling retreat than a harried sightseeing tour, my co-worker Vivian and I, who were there as the young *America* staff members, spent every moment of the day socializing with the pilgrims at meals, counting passengers on the tour bus, lending a supportive arm to the slower walkers over the cobblestones, and, for my part, explaining at least fifty times what exactly a podcast was and how to download one. It was only at the very end of the pilgrimage, the day we visited the Tomb of the Holy Sepulcher, which is believed to be the site of Jesus's Crucifixion and Resurrection, that I finally had a moment of quiet.

That new resolve I had been hoping for finally came in two breakthroughs.

First, exhausted emotionally and mentally by the trip, and physically by my lack of sleep, having spent the last few hours trying to hold my ground as impatient pilgrims from other groups shoved us and tried to cut in line, I finally collapsed kneeling with my hands and head resting on the rock that covers Christ's tomb for my allotted three seconds. (Really, they have someone with a stopwatch there telling people to keep it moving.) Still, it was enough time for me to feel a swell of energy and consolation coming from the tomb and washing over me, and to hear God telling me unmistakably: "Here is your only hope."

I knew exactly what this message meant. Two weeks before, in Montréal, I'd read two quotations from one of my favorite Catholic writers, Madeleine Delbrêl, that Sylvester had given me: "For the Gospel to reveal its mystery, no special setting, no advanced education, no particular technique is required. All it needs is a soul bowed down in adoration and a heart stripped of trust in all things human." Here I was, physically bowed down, adoring, at the site of the Resurrection, having no hope left in the human institution of the church. The consensus among commentators was that nothing would come from the Vatican's abuse summit. Even the holiest site in Christianity was a place filled with aggressive pilgrims, where fights broke out over who could see the tomb first. The church building itself is divvied up between Christian factions who depend on a fragile status quo to prevent literal wars from breaking out.

The second quotation was, "Unless you take this little book of the Gospel in your hand with the determination of a person who is holding onto his very last hope, you will neither be able to figure it out nor receive its message." Here was my last hope. Here was the one and only thing that made this putrid world, this filth-soaked institution, worth anything: the fact that, despite it all, despite humanity literally killing God Incarnate, God decided we were worth saving, and he rose again for us.

Twenty minutes after I laid my hands on Jesus's empty tomb, we were piled into a side chapel a few meters away for Mass. My colleague Fr. James Martin, who gave this retreat every year based on his book *Jesus: A Pilgrimage,* was the celebrant, and each time we'd gotten a chance to talk that week, we both told each other that the retreat had been spiritually dry. Neither Jim nor I had been able to connect with God in the way we had wanted to.

When celebrating Mass in the Holy Land, it's customary to read the Gospel reading that took place at the particular location of the Mass. So Jim picked up the lectionary and began to read St. John's account of the Resurrection—the one where Jesus appears to Mary Magdalene first.

As he read, I thought about what I'd learned about Mary Magdalene that week: that the idea that she was a prostitute only took shape around the third century, and that her reputation in the early church was one of a wealthy and reliable supporter of the community. Her name, Magdalene, might not even refer to Magdala being her hometown—it could also have been a descriptor of her character, meaning "tower."

All week, Mary Magdalene had been there, present in the Gospels that we read in each of the places we went. Along the Via Dolorosa, the Way of the Cross in Jerusalem, she had been there, even when the male disciples—even Peter, the church's rock—had run away. Mary Magdalene, the tower, never left; she was also never given her due. Excavation and construction of a church at Magdala had only begun in recent years, and the only image of Mary Magdalene in the church there was a mosaic of her surrounded by snakes, meant to represent the seven demons being driven out of her, a story that may not even have been about her to begin with. There was no sign of the Mary Magdalene who stayed with Jesus, proclaimed the Resurrection, or supported the early church. Even the church building was called "Duc in Altum" ("Put out into the deep"), something Jesus had said to Peter, not Mary Magdalene.

Seeing Mary Magdalene portrayed at her worst, with the seven demons, in a church that should honor her, angered me and some of the other women pilgrims. We spoke about it in our faith-sharing session that night: how our anger had made it difficult to pray there and in the visits to other cities that afternoon; how all we wanted to talk to God about was how Mary Magdalene had been given short shrift in her hometown. My spiritual dryness, it turned out, wasn't just the result of being exhausted and distracted by work. It was also caused by the anger and frustration that had been building up in me since Rome, which I hadn't yet had the chance to bring to God and just cry and yell about, the way I had in Montréal.

Jim, reading the Easter story at the Holy Sepulcher, began to choke up. Mary Magdalene was there, seeing the risen Jesus but thinking he was the gardener. She demanded to know what had happened to Jesus's body. I imagined myself in her shoes: bereaved, missing my dearest friend, whom I'd spent the last three years traveling with and learning from—and now, absolutely incensed that after his violent execution, which I had witnessed, his body was missing. I thought of when I had lost people I loved, and how the only thing I wanted to hear was their voice saying my name again, in the way that only they could. And how Jesus was right there, about to give that to her, how after literally going through hell and back, she was the first one he wanted to see.

"Mariam!" Jim's voice cracked. Our eyes filled with tears at the same time. "Rabbouni!" he whispered her reply.

I couldn't stop crying—even today, that two-word exchange makes me tear up, because it was the two-word exchange that changed history.

Here is your only hope. Here is the exchange that makes this god-awful world worth living in.

Jesus tells Mary Magdalene to go tell the others. Jim imagines her running across town to tell them. I think, if I were her, I'd have taken it slow, trying to process what had just happened and how to tell the disciples. For those few minutes, long or short as that walk or run may have been, Mary Magdalene was the church. The whole church. She was the recipient and steward of the Gospel, the first one entrusted with the very same mission that the whole church has been entrusted with since that morning. No pope, no hierarchy, just one soon-to-be-ignored woman whom Jesus entrusted with the most decisive news in history, and the men—the ones who would become the popes and bishops and the justification for an all-male priesthood because "Jesus only chose men"—didn't believe her.

ø   ø   ø

YOU DON'T HAVE to read the story of Mary Magdalene as an argument for women's ordination. At the same time, we cannot ignore that Mary Magdalene was given a very real spiritual, evangelical authority: she was ordered to proclaim the Gospel. That has significant implications for the church— not least of which is raising the question, Why are women categorically not allowed to read the Gospel at Mass or to give a homily? Why do we have to call it a "reflection" and have it introduced by a priest?

The Catholic Church must reckon anew with the question of authority: Who exercises authority in the church, and how? Is that authority respected? Is it exercised with love, or has it become a power devoid of love? I think here about the bishops who were in a position of authority over the nuns working in their homes: Is having nuns clean their house an appropriate use of their authority? Does it respect the spiritual and teaching authority that those nuns have, which they hoped to exercise for the church when they discerned a call to religious life? And what consequences should there be for those who abuse the nuns' authority?

Any discussion of women's ordination needs to start from the story of Mary Magdalene and this question of authority. Ordaining women is not, as some argue, an easy fix for the problems of sexual abuse or even clericalism. At the same time, the argument against ordaining women because it will "clericalize" women or reinforce the idea that priests are superior to laypeople is not compelling unless the people who make that argument are actively working against clericalism in the male-only priesthood. In my experience, many aren't.

I see great potential in the synodal process and in Pope Francis's appointments of women—which are meant to set an example for dioceses around the world—as a starting point for dismantling clericalism. Likewise, the pope allowing women to be formally installed in liturgical ministries like lector and acolyte and the teaching ministry of catechist is a nod toward our God-given authority. My prayer is that this discussion of authority can be had in an honest, uninhibited, and discerning way, taking into account the full implications of Mary Magdalene's God-given mission.

So, no, against all odds, I did not return from my marathon trip to Montréal, Rome, and Israel as an atheist, but with new resolve. I'd collapsed onto the stone that covered God's tomb, bereft of hope "in all things human," as Madeleine Delbrêl wrote, and when I rose I listened to the Gospel reading, as she said, "with the determination of a person who is holding onto [her] very last hope." And I heard the Gospel anew: As the story of a woman whom Jesus so deeply loved that he entrusted her with the very message he had become incarnate to deliver—that death was defeated, that despite everything she'd experienced, even the literal execution of God, sin and evil did not ultimately win out. Life did, forever.

Emboldened by the grace of being trusted with that message, Mary Magdalene delivered it to the apostles who remained hiding in fear. They didn't believe her; it would take Jesus appearing to them himself, days later at Pentecost, before they worked up the courage to leave their hiding place and share the news themselves. That is, Jesus appeared and vindicated Mary Magdalene's witness.

Mary Magdalene's story is echoed in those of so many women I know: women who give everything to follow where they feel God is calling them, only to encounter unbelief and institutional inertia and sin—even, at times, from the successors of the apostles. At the Holy Sepulcher that day, I came to hear the Gospel story as a promise that God will vindicate these women's witness, and indeed the witness of all people who, despite remaining faithful to what God has asked them to do, find themselves disbelieved, opposed, or even abused by fellow Catholics. So I went back to New York, knowing the bullshit would continue but determined to stay the course.

CHAPTER 3

Schism in the Heart

I knew the priest was talking about me and my friends when he invited the congregation to stay after Latin Mass and pray a Rosary "for those who seek to destroy the church from within." It was nothing new: I get emails, DMs, and Twitter replies almost every day calling me a heretic, accusing me of doing the work of Satan or leading other Catholics into sin, or being a propagandist for feminism, the pope, and the devil—a trio that makes sense only in the deepest recesses of the Catholic internet.

I couldn't be all that angry, either: After all, I was only at Latin Mass that day because my fiancé had dared me to go. A couple of weeks before, in response to my complaining about traditionalists, Simon had said frankly: "You hate these people."

And he'd challenged me to do something about it.

"I dare you to go to Latin Mass every other week for the rest of the summer," he said.

It was only May. "Fine," I groaned.

I knew he was right. And I knew the solution he proposed was right, too. It's something the Jesuits call *agere contra*—"acting against." If a Jesuit is afraid of, say, working at a nursing home, his superior is likely to send him to do exactly that, because God probably has something to teach him through the experience.

That was how, on a stifling New York Sunday, I'd come to duck into a cold and dark stone church for the pre–Vatican II Tridentine Liturgy (called that because it was instituted after the Council of Trent in the sixteenth century, the Latin name for Trent being Tridentum), being invited to pray for my own conversion, that I wouldn't "destroy the church from within."

🍃 🍃 🍃

IT MIGHT SURPRISE anyone who's met me in the last few years that I used to be a regular Latin Mass attendee. Then again, it may not—I'm hardly the only person to have crossed the chasm from traditionalism to what I often call "social justice Catholicism," knowing it's a shorthand as unhelpful as any other nickname for the Catholic cultural-political divide. I'm also far from being the only one who gives lip service to the idea that this chasm should not exist, and that it is exaggerated in the United States, where the so-called liturgy wars are a symptom of the bigger "culture" war. What surprised me was how deep that chasm was within myself.

I wrote in the introduction to this book about my childhood proclivity for the mystical, how I was "haunted by God," to borrow a phrase from Dorothy Day. God was everywhere, immediately accessible, a comforting presence I could feel at any time if I took a moment, opened my heart, and became aware of it. It was a spirituality of deep love, wonder, and an easy, intimate contemplation. Uncomplicated.

Even as I've grown older and life has grown more complex, when God does poke a hole through the dark veil that divides us, he comes through clearly—like that day at the Holy Sepulcher. Deep down, the little mystic Colleen is still there.

That sense of God's beauty and mystery was what first drew me to the Latin Mass as a college freshman. I admit, though, I got a rough start. The first time I decided to go to Latin Mass, I donned my Easter dress, a lovely white lace sleeveless thing that went down to my knees, and rode my rusted red Schwinn to St. Patrick's, the imposing white concrete church in New Orleans's arts district. Despite its modern-looking exterior, the inside was old-school, all lined with dark wood paneling. Three tall paintings of biblical scenes featuring billowy-robed figures rose high behind an ornate ten-foot altarpiece that itself looked like a miniature church; gold light shone out of the tiny stained-glass windows above the tabernacle at its base, a sort of mirror image of the stained-glass window dome that forms the roof of the cathedral's sanctuary.

I'd been advised by some of my friends who were Latin Mass regulars to show up early, because the 10:15 start time referred to the technical start of the liturgy—the sprinkling rite, or asperges—which comes a few minutes into the celebration, after the opening hymn. Showing up well before even then, I decided to get in the confession line. The confessional was a big carved wooden box like the ones you see in the movies, where the priest sits behind a screen and the penitent kneels. I'd never been in one before. In fact, I'd never even been to confession behind a screen; I always preferred to sit facing the priest and have a conversation: half confession, half advice on how I could do better going forward.

The person in front of me disappeared into one side of the box. Seeing an open curtain on the other side, I walked in, closed it, and knelt down facing the screen. I couldn't see or hear the priest. I sat in silence for a couple of minutes. *Should I just . . . start?* I wondered. I didn't want to seem like a newbie, though, and figured the priest was likely getting impatient if he was, in fact, waiting for me. So I launched into it. "Bless me, Father, for I have sinned. . . ."

About three-quarters of the way through my confession, the priest slid open the screen. "Go ahead." *Oh, shit.* He'd been hearing someone else's confession the whole time, and I'd been talking to a wood board. My cheeks flushed. Had he heard me? How embarrassing. I confessed again, then went to find a seat with my friends.

The Mass was beautiful, in the way that a piece of art you don't really understand is. It was exotic to me, who had grown up in St. Louis, where the St. Louis Jesuits' folksy guitar hymns from the 1970s still had a hold on most parish music directors, some of whom had been in the Jesuits' choir back in the day. As is common in New Orleans churches, the musicians at this Mass were classically trained; they sang gorgeous polyphonies while the altar boys swung smoking thuribles. My friends showed me how to follow along with the English translation in the missal, and I tried my best to pronounce the Latin in the prayers that the congregation was supposed to say.

Still, I felt that I stuck out like a sore thumb. I knew I would be one of the few women not wearing a mantilla, a lace veil covering my hair, but I thought that my Easter dress would help me blend in. Instead, I realized halfway through the Mass that I was the only woman with my shoulders showing. My nicest, most churchy dress was, I realized in horror, slutty by Latin Mass standards.

AFTER A FEW weeks of practice, I stopped feeling so out of place and could focus more on the Mass than on my own insecurities. I came to love biking down the dirty, potholed streets in the harsh sun and emerging into the cool, beautiful church. It was like a different world. I have always felt close to God when I sing, especially sacred music, and learning the Latin chants added a new sense of beauty and mystery and transcendence to my prayer. I started meeting friends in an echoey concrete art gallery on campus most weeknights to chant compline—the Liturgy of the Hours' nighttime prayer—in Latin before bed. Though it was a practice new to me, it felt homey and familiar: singing with friends, feeling like my heart itself was rising and falling with the cadence of the music, hearing the reverberations that gave our voices more life than we could on our own. It was mystical, not only in the childlike way I loved, but in an intellectual way, too, knowing that the songs we chanted were chanted in monasteries around the world, rippling across the time zones, wrapping the world in sacred song.

For the better part of two years, I went to Latin Mass fairly regularly—though not every week, because I had commitments to sing at the Sunday night student Mass at my university. I went to Eucharistic Adoration at a nearby chapel every morning and chanted compline almost every night. The summer after sophomore year, I visited different Carmelite communities, discerning whether there was a place for me in the order of great mystics like Teresa of Avila and John of the Cross. That fall, I moved to Switzerland for a semester abroad and found myself living on Route Mont-Carmel, going to Mass in French—a language I'd learned since I was little—in the chapel of a convent of Carmelite brothers. There, my favorite of the brothers, Emmanuel-Marie, led us all in singing hymns a cappella, with these haunting harmonies French Catholics learn to sing as children. Although I had discerned that God was not calling me to be a nun, I took the presence of Carmel in my street name and my parish as a sign that God wanted me connected to the order in some way.

I kept my unfailing sense of the mystical: I hiked out to La Valsainte, a silent Carthusian monastery in the middle of a breathtaking valley in the Alps, and tried to quiet my thoughts enough to feel God's presence the whole time. I enrolled in the brown scapular: I started wearing a little rough piece of fabric around my neck which was meant to be a tiny version of a Carmelite habit. There are lots of old superstitions about scapulars, like that you can't be burned or drowned while wearing one. I didn't believe any of that, but every time I felt the scratchy fabric against my chest or back, I thought of God and was reminded of the enrollment ceremony I did in the Carmelites' chapel, where I sang my favorite Latin chant, St. Hildegard of Bingen's "Alma Redemptoris Mater," my voice echoing off the thin, translucent walls that the sun shone through. To this day, when I pray, I still imagine myself in that chapel.

⁂

MY LAST MONTH in Switzerland, I got a text from my sister. "Did you hear about Christina?" "No," I texted back. "What about her?"

Christina was one of my dearest friends in high school. She was bright and cheerful; at that point she was in an accelerated five-year university program to become a pharmacist. Christina was smart and wanted to use her abilities to help people. Even during the program, she would send me cute animal pictures just to stay in touch. Whatever Claire was texting me about, I assumed it was good news.

"She died," Claire texted back. "They brought us all in for an assembly at school and told us."

I couldn't tell you what happened next. I had no idea what had happened to Christina, and no one I asked had answers. Was it a drunk driver? Some accident? I wandered around my Swiss town like a zombie, imagining what could have happened to her, waiting for any update from friends at home, but hearing nothing. I replayed my memories of her in my head and took down the one picture of her I'd brought to Switzerland; I started carrying it in my coat pocket. I searched online for plane tickets to America and begged my parents to fly me back for the funeral, but they insisted we couldn't afford it.

It so happened that the evening I landed in my hometown, St. Louis, the day of my long-scheduled flight, was the day of Christina's wake. My best friend, Alyssa, happened to be at the baggage claim to pick someone else up and had just come from the viewing. "It was closed casket," she said. "They won't tell us how she died, but . . ."

By that point, it had been weeks, and the silence from anyone who might have known how Christina died could only mean one thing. She was under so much stress in her program, and we knew her sister struggled with depression. . . . Still, without any confirmation, I reflexively stopped myself from thinking about it. I still had plausible deniability.

The next morning, at the funeral, the priest began his homily: "We never know why people choose to take their own lives." I didn't hear the rest. The confirmation that Christina had killed herself broke something open in me. I sobbed through the homily and the rest of the Mass; I tried to get it under control, but the tears and grief kept coming, crashing over me in a way that hadn't even happened when I'd first heard the news. The funeral luncheon was a teary blur. I went to Alyssa's house with some other friends after;

we sat on the floor of her childhood bedroom in our black funeral clothes, taking pulls of a shitty whiskey someone had been saving for a party.

◊ ◊ ◊

BACK AT LOYOLA, I took off my scapular and mostly avoided the chapel where I used to pray every day. I certainly couldn't go back to Latin Mass; I could barely go to regular Mass, though I managed to sometimes. I was the lead reporter on the student paper the semester after Christina died, and the night before school started, we learned that a student had died by suicide. Two others who lived on campus died of fentanyl overdoses—one accidental, one that seemed intentional—within the following weeks, and then a young professor died by suicide. I reported on all of them, watching two of the students' bodies wheeled out of the dorms in body bags, thinking about Christina being wheeled out of her own dorm. I drank a lot more and kept my distance from anything that smelled like traditional Catholicism.

I knew the long-standing Catholic teaching was that suicide was a mortal sin—that anyone who died that way was in hell. And even though the priest at Christina's funeral had offered a more compassionate view, that she wasn't entirely at fault for something her depression had led her to do, which is what the church has taught since 1992, I didn't know the teaching had changed. (The church began allowing people who died by suicide to have Catholic funerals in the 1980s.)

Looking back now, I get that the traditional teaching against suicide is a teaching *for* the value of a human life—of Christina's life, a value I knew firsthand was immeasurable. (God, I still miss my friend.) The problem is, that was also a teaching of condemnation, and although the pastor at Christina's funeral tried to explain that suicide was not something for which she was entirely guilty—that she was not necessarily damned (Can you imagine believing your friend is cut off from the love of God forever?)—I feared that the traditionalists I'd been spending so much time around, whose mysterious and beautiful worship I loved, didn't support that kind of wiggle room in church teaching. They were very concerned about anyone "watering down" the faith.

I don't think that fear was entirely unfounded. I'd seen this dynamic play out over the previous two years, as Pope Francis brought his experience as a Jesuit spiritual director to the papacy. Jesuits, if you aren't familiar, are trained in what they call discernment—paying close attention to where "the good spirit" (God) and "the evil spirit" (Satan) are moving in our lives, in our thoughts and emotions and desires. It's an approach that gives a lot of weight to one's conscience: not in a "you can do whatever you want" way but in a way that acknowledges that God has a unique relationship with each of us and that no two life situations are the same. Discernment is figuring out what God is asking you to do in the midst of the unique messiness of your life—which may look different from what someone else in a similar situation is called to do.

This approach is a big change for Catholics who were basically used to being told what to do—"pay, pray, and obey," to use a trite slogan. So when Pope Francis was elected and, a few months later, said that if a gay priest is seeking God with a sincere heart, "Who am I to judge?," it shocked a lot of people, Catholic or not. "Who is he to judge? He's the pope! He has every right to judge!" (And besides, some would point out, there shouldn't even be gay priests according to church teaching, because gay men are not supposed to be admitted to seminary.)[1] But Francis recognized that God could still be at work in the life of a priest who's attracted to men.

A couple of years later, Pope Francis expressed an openness to letting Catholics who were divorced and remarried receive Communion.[2] Up to now, the teaching had been strict: If you remarried after a divorce and didn't get your first marriage annulled by a church tribunal (a long and arduous process that Francis also shortened),[3] you were actively committing adultery, "persevering in sin," and couldn't receive Communion. This was, of course, heartbreaking for many Catholics whose first marriages hadn't worked out for whatever reason and who wanted to be able to receive God in the Eucharist. My mom remembers how her grandfather never went to Communion because of this. He was a devoted and devout Catholic father, but because his first marriage had failed, his new family was illegitimate in the church's eyes. Most divorced and remarried people these days receive Communion anyway, or go to an Episcopal church, or stop going to church at all, but for those who were committed to following the letter of the law, it meant a permanent ban from Communion.

Pope Francis would ultimately hold a two-session synod (a meeting of bishops and other experts) on the family, issuing a teaching document afterward, in 2016, that mentioned the Communion issue in a footnote.[4] In it, he said that pastors could work one-on-one with divorced members of their congregations to discern whether God was calling them back to the sacrament, and whether they needed to make any changes in their lives to make that possible. It might not, in all cases, be necessary or even good for the remarried spouses to separate or stop having sex—either of these could be detrimental to the new family they had created.

Still, this perceived moral laxity on the pope's part caused an uproar among traditionalists. Four cardinals issued *dubia* (literally, "doubts," a set of yes-or-no questions challenging the pope's teaching),[5] a group of conservative theologians likewise issued a "filial correction" of the pope,[6] and it became the smoking gun that Francis's critics could point to as evidence that he was, to borrow a phrase from that priest at Latin Mass, "destroying the church from within." Never mind that he was suggesting that pastors employ with their congregants an almost five-hundred-year-old tradition of prayerful discernment that was established by one of the church's most influential saints.

As someone who covers Catholic news, I've unfortunately seen up close how the backlash to the footnote on Communion in "Amoris Laetitia" ("The Joy of Love") kicked off—or at least dramatically accelerated—a resistance to Pope Francis that runs the gamut from those who ignore him and are quietly waiting for his pontificate to end to those who believe he is an antipope or even the Antichrist, beliefs held by a small group of Catholics ranging from laypeople up to bishops. The resistance, I believe, is rooted in an uneasiness about how church teaching intersects with the messiness of human life. Whereas in past generations, popes in their teaching laid out a beautiful ideal (like, for example, John Paul II's "theology of the body") for Catholics to strive for, Pope Francis acknowledges that there are many situations in which the messiness of our lives makes that ideal unattainable. In the past, people in such situations would have run up against the limits of the church's ministry, like my great-grandpa. Pope Francis believes that people whose lives are messier than the church's ideal still deserve to be accompanied and ministered to, and helped to discern how they can participate in the church's life rather than being alienated from it.

This backlash to Pope Francis's more pastoral teaching was growing in the U.S. Catholic Church at the same time that I was grappling with Christina's death and my beliefs about what happened to her after she died, and I knew that those who were most opposed to Pope Francis's approach—an approach that would not condemn Christina but allowed that she could still reach heaven—were often the same people who most vocally advocated for the Latin Mass.

I feared that if I went back to Latin Mass, I might encounter an attitude of condemnation rather than consolation there. It wasn't unimaginable that the priest might deliver a homily that touched on suicide and state absolutely that those who took their own lives were in hell. After my breakdown at Christina's funeral, I wasn't sure I could take hearing that from a pulpit. I also knew I would want to process my grief with my church community, and I dreaded the idea that I might mention Christina's death to someone and then have to watch as they tried to find something to say that wouldn't imply she was no longer suffering, because they believed she was.

Most important, I knew that deep down, I simply did not believe the traditional teaching. It didn't align with my experience of God as forgiving and loving. And I felt that God had confirmed this for me one night, months after Christina's death. I'd gone on a walk to pray and wandered up to the top floor of a parking garage. It was dark, and the moon was a gold crescent—the symbol of the Catholic school we'd attended together. A strong wind was whipping around me, and when it calmed, I felt Christina there with me, a peaceful, comforting presence. I closed my eyes and felt her hug me, just like she used to. She told me she was going to be okay. I believed her.

ø ø ø

IT ISN'T FAIR that I assumed the people at Latin Mass would believe without exception that Christina was doomed to suffer forever. But over the following years, as the chasm between American traditionalists and "Vatican II" Catholics grew and was exacerbated, as every divide was, by the 2016 election, I felt affirmed that avoiding Latin Mass had been the right choice. A number of alt-right figures whose views I found reprehensible—Steve Bannon, Milo Yiannopolous— had declared themselves "Latin Mass" Catholics, and Archbishop Viganò, who had staged the unsuccessful coup against Pope Francis, was now writing letters to President Trump, declaring that there was a "deep state" conspiracy to elect Joe Biden, just as there had been a "deep church" behind Francis's election.[7]

At the same time, I'd drifted into the opposite camp of American Catholics. A few months after Christina died and I had abandoned Latin Mass, I was sitting in a meeting of the student newspaper's editorial board when I got a *New York Times* alert that said that Jesuit poet, priest, and antiwar activist Daniel Berrigan had died. I'd never heard of Dan, as I now call him, but reading his obituary led me down a rabbit hole of researching twentieth-century Catholic peace and justice activism. I discovered Dorothy Day and her Gospel-inspired nonviolence and read about Oscar Romero and the Jesuits and churchwomen of El Salvador who had worked for social justice and been killed for their efforts. I started asking around: "Is anyone still doing anything like this?" and was introduced to the Catholic Workers and Catholic activists who were working for a variety of social justice causes. I went with one such group to the Louisiana State Penitentiary at Angola, the country's largest maximum-security prison, to meet inmates, and started writing articles on criminal justice reform. With another group, I went to a protest led by a Jesuit priest in one of

New Orleans's aboveground cemeteries—a memorial service for all the people who would die if Louisiana cut its Medicaid expansion program. I started going to Mass with a group of old Catholic hippies in an unfussy chapel in Loyola's humanities building.

After graduation, I moved to New York to work at the Jesuit magazine *America,* and they put me up in a dorm next door to St. Paul the Apostle, a Paulist church on West Sixtieth Street. The parish is known for its LGBT ministry, Out at St. Paul, and I loved going to the 5:15 p.m. young adult Mass there, where off-duty Broadway performers and Julliard students sang old "guitar Mass" hymns with a level of musicianship I'd never encountered. It was at St. Paul's that I began to heal from Christina's death, without really trying to. In the Eucharistic prayer, when we asked God to remember those who had died, I thought of her; I felt the sting of grief, but also the comfort of not being alone in my grief. I was surrounded by other people just like me, around my age, who were bringing their own pains—some of them caused or exacerbated by the church—and laying them out before God in our prayer. After Communion, the instrumentalists would often cut out, leaving the singers a cappella, and we would all be carrying the nostalgic hymns together, holding one another's voices up with our own. It was impossible to feel alone.

My favorite part of Mass at St. Paul's was an unexpectedly old-school twist: At the end of Mass, before the closing hymn, we would all chant the Salve Regina together in Latin. It was the traditional song I loved, but without the traditionalism that I now found intolerable. It felt freeing to sing it again.

Likewise, I'd started dropping in for evening vespers at the Catholic Worker downtown from time to time. Although it wasn't quite the Latin compline chanting I'd once done nightly, there was something deeply moving about praying the psalms in the evening with men and women who had given up their possessions and livelihoods to live in voluntary poverty and community with the poorest people in New York, asking nothing in return. These people were the real deal, and praying with them showed me how even their radical work for peace and justice was rooted in an ancient prayer tradition—the same words were being prayed at the same time at silent Carthusian monasteries as in this basement cafeteria papered with pictures of Gandhi and Jesus and Guantánamo Bay.

Finding these faith communities of a decidedly progressive political bent helped me heal from Christina's death and slowly return to some of the more traditional practices I'd run away from. And as I became more open to those practices, I worked up the courage to try again with a more traditional community—only to be met with the combative brand of traditionalism that had been brewing in the years since the Trump election.

✿ ✿ ✿

I'D BEEN PRAYING more deeply, stealing into St. Paul's before work or St. Patrick's Cathedral after, and I decided it was time to give the Carmelites another shot. I'd lost contact with them after I left Switzerland, but I was (and still am) serious about joining the third order, so I reached out to their New York group and started attending meetings once a month in a church basement downtown. It was just a short walk from the Catholic Worker, but it felt worlds apart.

The meetings began with a catechesis and group reflections on the "rule" of the third order—the document that outlines the responsibilities of a lay Carmelite, how often they pray, how often they meet, and guidelines for how they should live. After that was lunch, which, since most of the members had known one another for years, usually involved me, the newbie, being asked a lot of questions.

It only ever took a couple of minutes for my tablemates to find out I worked for the Jesuits at *America,* and another minute to put together that I worked closely with Fr. James Martin. Every time, they would urge me to "correct" him or tell me how scandalous his positions were. Even the more understanding people in the group believed he wanted to change church teaching to include marrying gay couples, which he's never said. Jim's writing—to the chagrin of activists who would like to see him go further—has never advocated a change in church teaching; he focuses entirely on the church and LGBT community having respect for one another rather than animosity. Still, it doesn't stop critics from protesting every talk he gives or every reflection he tweets. One time, they even organized a "get blocked by James Martin" campaign, where they tweeted increasingly mean comments at him on a day that he was undergoing chemo.

I toughed out the lunches for a few months, figuring the interest in Jim would wane, but it kept going. At every meeting, I got so much out of the catechesis and prayer and felt so drawn in by the Carmelite rule, then would have to spend all of lunchtime defending Jim, when what I really wanted to talk about was Carmel and the Carmelite saints and to feel a part of the community. I prayed about what to do and discerned that I would stop going to the meetings and try again another time, with another community. In the years since Christina had died and I'd left the Latin Mass, the chasm in the church had gotten bigger, and my drifting to one side had made me unable to tolerate the other.

That experience, and the news I was following about Viganò and Bannon, and the messages I was receiving online, all led to me complaining about the trads to Simon one afternoon. That led him to dare me to go back to Latin Mass, which led to me being invited to pray the Rosary "for the conversion of those who seek to destroy the church from within" and knowing it was about me, and Jim, and everyone else I worked with, and most of my friends.

At this point, I was already feeling defensive. I didn't want to do this dare, and part of me hoped that some person in the congregation would notice that even with my uncovered head and a dress that didn't reach my knees, I still knew all the Latin Mass responses by heart. I was still just as Catholic as they were, even if they thought I was lesser, or inferior, or a satanist-propagandist like my Twitter trolls always said. (You can see how this hatred distorts people's vision of others—it had spoiled mine as much as it had the trolls'.)

It got worse before it got better. When a phalanx of priests, deacons, subdeacons, and altar servers—only boys—emerged from the sacristy and processed to the sanctuary at the first Latin Mass I went back to, I felt my face turn red. When I realized that no women were allowed past the altar rail even though these tween altar boys were, I felt my hands tense up. I debated making a quick escape before Communion. "There is no way in hell," I told myself, "that I am going to go up and kneel at that rail and open my mouth obediently for this trad priest to put Communion on my tongue. There is no way." It felt embarrassing, humiliating, uncomfortably sexual. I hated the idea.

But if there was one thing that would be even more humiliating, it would be admitting defeat, telling Simon that I couldn't make it through a single Latin Mass anymore. So I stayed. I stayed to hear the Rosary invitation and the homily and the warbly voiced vocalist (there was no professional schola here, which admittedly decreased whatever sense of beauty or mystery I might have been able to scrounge up). I went up for Communion, and kneeled down, and opened my mouth, and blessed myself, and went back to pray. And, in spite of myself, I realized that this Communion was the same one they were receiving at my hippie Mass in New Orleans, and at St. Paul's, and in the Catholic Worker soup kitchen, where they used the meal prep table as an altar.

There we all were, the body of Christ, even when some parts of the body thought other parts would be better off amputated.

I tried again a couple of Sundays later, this time at St. Agnes, a whitewashed church less than a block from Grand Central. Already when I walked in, I liked it. The choir was warming up, and they were good. I was pretty sure I recognized them singing a Tomàs Luis de Victoria piece from the Middle Ages that I'd once done a school report on. The church's interior felt more welcoming, too: The walls were bright, and the windows high up in the vaulted ceiling let in some light, however improbably, from between the skyscrapers around it. There were gold hanging chandeliers and colorful images of saints behind the sanctuary, and two friendly couples with babies sat near me. Nobody minded when one family rolled in late.

What really won me over was when the priest mentioned during the parish announcements that he'd written a book that was available for sale—but if anyone couldn't spare $15, they were welcome to swing by the sacristy after Mass and he'd give them one for free.

This was a community, it seemed to me, that was characterized more by an openness to strangers and a desire to share beauty with them than by opposition to the world and "those who seek to destroy the church from within." It was traditionalist, yes, but the values were those I recognized from my old Latin Mass days, pre-Trump, pre-Viganò, pre–the constant talk of schism in the American church.

I returned to St. Agnes a few times for Latin Mass and

even took a friend there for Tenebrae, a dramatic service during Holy Week where a schola sings chants based on the Passion readings and loud noises—sometimes made by drumming on the pews, though I don't remember how they did it at this church—imitate the sound of the earthquake that's recounted in the Good Friday readings. Ultimately the few candles lighting the church are extinguished, and congregants leave in darkness. Even that time, the church was still lit from the windows, and people smiled warmly as they collected the programs after the service.

IN 2021, POPE Francis put restrictions on celebrations of the pre–Vatican II Mass.[8] The reason he cited in a note accompanying the decision was the exact chasm between "left" and "right" Catholicism that I'd experienced in myself.[9] While you could argue that it began after Vatican II, as people's liturgical preferences (at least in the United States) began aligning more with their secular political preferences,[10] it had without a doubt accelerated significantly in the preceding five years. The seemingly irreparable polarization that had divided populists and neoliberals the world over had torn deep into the church, too, with each side using their religious beliefs as proof that their political beliefs were incontrovertibly superior to others'.

For my podcast, *Inside the Vatican,* I interviewed a young man who was both a fan of Pope Francis and a lifelong Latin Mass attendee.[11] His family had been part of a special group that was given permission by John Paul II to celebrate the Latin Mass before Pope Benedict XVI opened it up more widely in 2007. This young man, Jonathan, didn't agree with Francis's restrictions, but he sympathized with the reasoning behind them.

"There are a number of events marking these last few years that have really affected my attitude or the way I think about many of the traditionalist community who attend the Latin Mass," he told me, choosing his words thoughtfully. "Not all of them, but there is definitely that vocal section of the community who has used the energy of certain key events," he said, citing the election of Pope Francis as a small one. Things really accelerated, he told me, with the 2016 presidential election and the 2018 abuse crisis. Then came Viganò's call for Francis to resign, which ultimately served as a litmus test for anyone's feelings about the pope. Viganò became a sort of figurehead leader for Pope Francis's critics, particularly in the United States, and Viganò then became an outspoken supporter of Donald Trump, writing missives to the president and the public endorsing the QAnon conspiracy theory and the "big lie" about the 2020 election.

"Viganò's involvement in the QAnon event was a huge contributor to this sort of new energy in the traditionalist movement," Jonathan said. "Oh, and all the politics around Covid, which I won't get into, but yeah, all of these things, it was just like one thing after another affected the traditionalist movement and accelerated certain trends . . . and turned it into something that I couldn't really be okay with anymore."

When we spoke in 2021, Jonathan was no longer regularly attending the Latin Mass. He'd gotten married and started attending and playing piano for the Vatican II Masses at his wife's parish. They were about to move to a new state, and he wasn't sure what Mass they would go to— in part because they didn't know how Francis's new restrictions on the Latin Mass would be applied.

It seems the tipping point for the pope himself was that the political divisions in the church had led to some Latin Mass devotees refusing to recognize that the Second Vatican Council had been legitimate at all—a big deal, since an ecumenical council like Vatican II is one of the highest teaching authorities in the church. He put in place guardrails so that priests who wanted to celebrate the Latin Mass had to get Vatican approval, and part of the approval criteria would be making sure they recognized the legitimacy of the council and weren't primarily motivated by an ideology to celebrate the old form of the Mass. Jonathan thought the move was too much;[12] I thought it was justified. It's now been applied rather unevenly: with bishops who were eager to clamp down on celebrations of the Latin Mass in their dioceses banning, in some cases, all of them, and others declaring that anyone who seeks permission to celebrate the Latin Mass will be granted it, at least by the bishop, if not by Rome. There are rumors that further restrictions are to come, but they haven't materialized as of this writing.

The speculation about a schism being imminent in the American church continues. Every once in a while, a commentator will accuse some bishop or layperson of having stepped over the line into schism, like when Bishop Joseph Strickland of Tyler, Texas, tweeted that Pope Francis was "undermining the deposit of faith." He was removed from his post a few months later. But as of now, no mainstream American Catholic has formally declared that they are in schism, nor has the Vatican. The pope's fiercest critics among the bishops might have been reassigned to less important roles, but they remain bishops in good standing, with the exception of the Italian Viganò, who was excommunicated in 2024 after being found guilty of schism and denying the legitimacy of Vatican II. Pope Francis is asked constantly about his American critics and even about schism, and he decries what he calls their "rigidity" and "indietrismo"—a word he invented to mean "backward-looking-ness."

"I am not afraid of schisms," he said in response to one of these questions during one of his signature freewheeling press conferences aboard the papal plane. "I pray they do not happen," he continued.[13]

I DON'T EXPECT ANY of the pope's American critics to formally declare that they are in schism, nor do I expect the Vatican to make a judgment about whether any of the critics besides Viganò have gone so far as to be in schism. But the soul-searching I did in forcing myself to go to Latin Mass over and over until I no longer hated it or the people around me there showed me that a "schism of the heart" is a reality that pervades more American Catholics than I think are willing to admit it. What do I mean by this? In the same way that Jesus talks about how one has already committed adultery "in the heart" just by thinking about another person lustfully—even if they never go so far as to cheat on their spouse with that person—one doesn't need to formally declare schism in order to be schismatic, in order to hold attitudes of being the "true" Catholic and believing others are lesser, of seeing one's coreligionists as enemies. These "schisms of the heart," although they aren't "real" schisms, are a spiritual and emotional reality that I have had to learn to chase down, persistently and often unsuccessfully acting against them (*agere contra*) within myself so that they don't grow.

CHAPTER 4

When Heroes Fall

One of the most impactful conversations in my life happened on a beat-up brown sofa in a dingy dorm room. My friend Katie had just returned from Ireland, where she'd gone to live for a year in a L'Arche community after finishing her degree in economics. Katie was smart, poised for a lucrative career, and decided to give it up to go live in community with people with developmental disabilities. The choice to "give it all up" to live with the poor was one I recognized from the stories of saints—and, admittedly, my understanding of what Katie had given up was probably also skewed by the extreme pressure I was feeling around my career prospects as I neared the end of college. Would I be able to pay my loans back and afford a place to live? Would I be able to find a job in journalism? If I didn't land at a prestigious publication right out of school, would I ever be able to climb to that level?

Katie's seeming immunity to those pressures intrigued me, showing me an interior freedom I lacked. I wanted to know what had driven her to do it and what she had learned. So I asked her.

She responded with her own question: "Have you heard of Jean Vanier?"

Vanier was the founder of L'Arche, a worldwide network of communities where people with developmental disabilities live alongside people without disabilities. In the L'Arche houses, the community members work together on the cleaning and the cooking, and many of the people with disabilities hold jobs outside of the house if they are able. They have a close community life, praying and having meals together, and although people can be in foul moods sometimes, as in any family, it seems the overwhelming emotion in most of the houses is joy.

Katie didn't bother telling me the foundation myth—how Jean Vanier had left behind a wealthy family and a military career to live with two disabled French men he had rescued from a mental asylum where they'd lived in appalling conditions, and how the community then grew all over the world. She skipped to explaining to me his central idea that had spoken to her: "Everyone is interested in climbing the ladder, gaining wealth or prestige or whatever, but Jean Vanier says that the true Christian response to the world is to intentionally climb down the ladder."

Like God did in the Incarnation.

This conversation sparked in me an obsession with humility. For years after this in my journals, which I have always written as conversations with God, the idea of humility and the phrase "climbing down the ladder" come up nearly every day. (Whether that virtue actually took hold in me is a different story. . . .) It was part of why I was so attracted to the Catholic Worker and other intentional Christian communities where people choose to live in voluntary poverty, forgoing all the things like wealth and prestige that I was obsessed with. It offered me a way to be a bit more gentle with myself, too: What really mattered wasn't getting a job at a respected publication. What mattered was being in solidarity and community with people who were rejected, who lacked those things, who Jesus never stopped talking about and spending time with.

Vanier became one of my personal heroes. I read many of his books and kept his essential writings on my bedside table. I watched documentaries about him, hung a photo of him on my desk, and listened to his long-form interview with Krista Tippett any time I had to travel more than an hour and a half somewhere.

He inspired me to spend my extra time serving the poor, working at a soup kitchen in New Orleans, visiting old folks who had no families with Sant'Egidio in New York, handing out soup and sandwiches to homeless folks around Grand Central, volunteering at the Catholic Worker. I grew to love his idea, too, of a God who is hurt, and how it is God crying out from every wounded person (that is, every person), "Will you love me? Will you be my friend?"

When Jean Vanier died in May 2019, I watched his funeral streaming on my phone while I walked to the train. I listened to the eulogies on the platform and cried as we pulled into Grand Central watching the L'Arche community members walk down the aisle throwing orange peels—

oranges were Jean's favorite snack—into the congregation like flower girls at a wedding.

I wrote Vanier's obituary for *America* and did an interview about his death with Tina Bovermann, a spokeswoman for L'Arche USA, the last two of several articles and videos I'd done extolling Vanier's virtues, trying to spread his message that had changed my life on that dusty couch in New Orleans.

Less than a year later, I'd view it all with disdain.

✿ ✿ ✿

I WAS HOME VISITING my parents on February 22, 2020, when the news broke that Jean Vanier had been credibly accused of sexually abusing six non-disabled women at the first L'Arche house in Trosly-Breuil, France. It was spiritual abuse, not just sexual: in one-on-one spiritual direction, a context in which the directee is often very vulnerable and, to an extent, malleable, Vanier had pushed the incestuous idea that Jesus and Mary had a sexual relationship (*what the fuck?*) and that these women should have sex with him to emulate that relationship.

My journalistic and spiritual mind sometimes work sequestered from each other—I put away the spiritual and emotional in favor of getting the news reported and my story filed; only later will I open the box I'd put my emotions away in. My spiritual side is more emotional; my journalistic side is analytical, calm in a crisis, focused until the job is done. But that day, both sides were working in tandem: I needed to write, to make sense of this for myself, to analyze the news for my readers, to start processing what the hell this meant for me and for everyone else who had been so deeply moved and influenced by Jean Vanier.

I felt stupid. By now, I'd seen this happen so many times with Catholic leaders: Someone who is universally loved and respected is revealed to have been an abuser or to have turned a blind eye to abuse. The McCarrick scandal was still fresh at that point: a charismatic cardinal—someone who was friendly and rose through the ranks without becoming an ideologue, who brought in funds and vocations—had, it turned out, been grooming and molesting young seminarians for decades. And he was promoted over and over by John Paul II, who had known about the allegations and done nothing.

The first Vatican news story I have any memory of was the death of John Paul. I remember watching footage from the funeral on TV, and my fourth-grade teacher telling us that the signs that said "Santo Subito!" meant that people wanted the pope to be named a saint. More than a decade later, in college, I'd stay up late to watch the live stream of John Paul's canonization Mass. And a few years later, I'd hold my head in my hands, exhausted, as I paged through the seven-hundred-page report on McCarrick's rise that made clear now-Saint John Paul knew about McCarrick's abuse and chose not to believe the facts.

Had I really been stupid enough, after those cases, to think anyone could be beyond reproach?

And what did it mean for my credibility as a journalist that I'd been so blind? I'd covered Vanier almost completely uncritically for years, even though I knew that his spiritual mentor, Fr. Thomas Philippe, was a sexual abuser censured by the Vatican.[1] Yet Vanier remained close with Philippe, and Philippe was around the L'Arche community. I should have looked into that, been more skeptical about that relationship.

That lack of critical thinking, on the part of all of the people who had been unquestioning admirers of Vanier, had put Vanier's victims in the awful position of having to hear their abuser called a "living saint" ad nauseam. No wonder most of them waited until he had died to come forward. Maybe they were also worried about what would happen to L'Arche if they spoke out.

Looking ahead, I wrote, that critical thinking that I and many others had neglected was going to be even more important. It would be important for L'Arche, as they reckoned with how to distinguish the organization from its founder, and it would be important for ordinary people who had admired Jean, as we grappled with how to separate the profound good from the evil he had done.

As I wrestled with that myself—the question of to what extent the goodness and evil of one single person could be disentangled—I found myself struggling with the question of holiness. What did it mean to be a holy person? I'd long thought of Jean Vanier as a saint, and the evil he committed did not undo the good he had done. All the things that made him holy in my eyes were still there, but now they were stained by this abuse and spiritual manipulation. So, surely he wasn't a saint anymore, was he?

I started to question my own understanding of what a

saint was. I realized that I'd come to think of saints as more or less perfect people, which wasn't right. The theological definition I'd been taught was that a lowercase-*s* saint, that is, someone who isn't canonized, is anyone who is in heaven. And determining where Jean Vanier or anyone else was spending eternity was definitely above my pay grade. If I were to make those judgments, what, then, would make me any different from the Westboro Baptist Church members on the street corner telling people they're going to hell? I want to believe, deep down, that hell is empty, that everyone has a chance to reconcile with God and to be purged of their sins before entering heaven. It's old-school, even medieval, but I really do believe it; in fact, I find it hopeful. *Purgatorio* is my favorite book of the *Divine Comedy*.

I wrote in that initial piece reacting to the revelations that I wouldn't speculate about any conversion Vanier might have undergone, before or after his death. "I can no longer in good conscience call Jean Vanier a saint," I wrote,

> but I cannot accept the disturbing truth about him as proof, as some have understood it, that sanctity does not exist. Rather, I think it challenges us to consider our own and others' simultaneous capacity for profound goodness and evil, to seek models of holiness away from the world's spotlight and to pursue holiness ourselves far from the spotlight, at the bottom of the ladder.[2]

This rethinking of sainthood was something I had been kneading over in my mind a lot. Around the same time, in

February 2020, I'd found out that St. Rose Philippine Duchesne, who had founded the school in St. Charles, Missouri, I'd attended for ten years, and in whose shrine I had first come to care about my faith, had owned at least one slave while she was working in the United States as a missionary. That spring, I attended a meeting with some of the nuns from St. Philippine's order and sat with them as they discussed how to teach their students about her as a saint while being truthful about her slaveholding.

We talked about how we've put saints on such a pedestal that "saint" has become synonymous, colloquially, with "perfect person." It's understandable that we'd gotten used to simplifying it that way when teaching little kids, but we needed to help the older kids develop a more mature and honest understanding of the saints as people who had done good things and bad things, rebelled against certain sinful systems, and been complicit in others. We needed an idea of sainthood that was honest about that.

My piece reacting to the Vanier news, it turned out, hit home for many people. I got thirty or so emails about it in the next couple of days, people sharing their own disillusionment and experiences. One I remember well was from a man named John who told me that he'd been so disturbed, while he was getting sober, to learn that some of the men in his Alcoholics Anonymous group still did horrible things, like beat their kids, even though they'd gotten sober. These were guys he'd looked up to as role models. His disillusionment with them and his hunt for reliable role models brought him "back to the Church," he wrote me. "Back to the Church via the Legionaries of Christ. Hahahahahaha." (The Legionaries are an order of priests, often attractive and charismatic, who were rocked by an enormous scandal when it was revealed that their founder, Father Marcial Maciel, had had multiple affairs, fathered many children, had long-term drug addictions, and that no one in the Vatican had intervened because he was such a good fundraiser. There was a mass exodus from the order after the scandal broke.)

"Here's the drill," John continued. "The only one who will not disappoint us is Jesus. As they say, 'Love many, trust few, always row your own canoe.' Keep the Faith."

I LISTENED: I KEPT the faith, kept my work-in-progress belief in holiness as something more complicated than perfection, but I became very, very cautious about whom I looked up to. A month after the Vanier news broke, I pulled out of reviewing a documentary about another famous Catholic whom people often call a living saint. I didn't want to be burned again.

It was a valuable lesson if one I learned the hard way: Even the people who seem the best are still only human. No one is above criticism. I tried to incorporate that both into my reporting and in how I think about people. For example, I cover Pope Francis a lot, and it's no secret that I am generally supportive of his vision for the church. But since that initial Vanier report, I've been more careful, not that I think Pope Francis has manipulated or abused people the way Vanier has, but being honest about his shortcomings, voicing criticisms when I have them, and asking tough questions even if they might weaken people's support for an otherwise good initiative he has taken.

MAYBE THAT COMES off as a very negative way to see the world, but I see it as honesty, and even humility. I have to be humble enough to admit that I don't know everything about a person, that my judgment of character is often flawed. Trying to be honest with myself about the fact that every person is human, that none of my heroes are above falling, that you never know what might be going on behind the scenes, has helped me to see my role models as people, still.

It's also, conversely, reminded me that villains are people, too: that "hero" and "villain" as nouns are rarely accurate; that adjectives like "heroic" or "villainous" or "evil" are more accurate; and that they generally apply to a person's actions more than a person himself or herself. It's reminded me that evil, as Hannah Arendt famously wrote, is banal: it's something all of us far too readily participate in. That doesn't, however, mean certain evils are not extraordinary—after all, Arendt used that phrase covering the trial of Adolf Eichmann, one of the primary organizers of the Holocaust. A realistic view of evil also means a more realistic view of the gravity of certain evils. In Jean Vanier's case, it meant that I could take an honest view of both the great good and the great harm he had done.

It was a lesson that has continued to prove important when other stories like this one have come out. And they have kept coming.

☙ ☙ ☙

IN FEBRUARY 2023, L'Arche issued an 873-page report on Vanier. They had commissioned a third-party investigator to produce a report on abuse in L'Arche after the six women had come forward with their allegations against him. Its revelations were even more shocking than the first round.

To put it succinctly: Not only did Jean Vanier know about Fr. Thomas Philippe's abuse, but the weird Jesus-Mary incest stuff had actually come from Fr. Philippe, who himself was a victim of childhood sexual abuse and whose brother had also become a notorious abuser-priest. The whole community of young Catholics around Fr. Philippe, including Vanier, had adopted this bizarre, incestuous spirituality and the sexual practices that came with it, and when the Vatican censured Philippe, the community had to disperse. However, as is the case with so many Vatican interventions that start out well, there was not enough follow-up enforcement. So several from the community regrouped, and Vanier founded L'Arche, after visiting that mental asylum with Philippe, as a cover under which to reunite them.

The report says that the main reason Vanier's plan to reunite his incestuous sex cult failed was that L'Arche was "quickly joined and overtaken by a large number of people who were completely foreign to [the sex cult] and who, in turn, assumed the foundation project with different intentions and values."[3] Basically, the good people who genuinely wanted to live in community with and in service to disabled people so vastly outnumbered the sex-cult people that

L'Arche grew and grew and did tons of good, despite the rot at its founding.

AFTER THE 2020 Vanier revelations, L'Arche released a statement saying they were going to have to figure out how to tell L'Arche's founding story while being honest about the charismatic yet duplicitous figure of Jean Vanier. (I've been thoroughly impressed with the transparency they've shown through all of this.) But I think that sentence from the report—about too many good people joining too quickly—is the kind of founding story they can be proud of.

I took down my picture of Jean Vanier soon after the 2020 revelations came out. I debated, too, whether I should take down the pictures next to his of two other people I admired—Dorothy Day and Madeleine Delbrêl, both laywomen on the path to being canonized saints. I kept them up, but the office shut down for Covid soon after, and when I moved to New Orleans during the pandemic and set up an office at home, I didn't put their photos back up.

I still deeply admire Dorothy and Madeleine, and I write about them often. But I'm more cautious with myself now about how much of a pedestal I'll put my Catholic heroes on. The Jesuit anti-war activist Dan Berrigan is a hero of mine, for example, and I've gone on supporting his work, but not uncritically. I joined the steering committee of the Daniel Berrigan Collective, but only after realizing that the other members were people who really knew Dan, who were honest about his flaws. At the events we put on, people inspired by Dan's work are honest about where their views diverge from his. There is no reverential cone of silence.

In late 2020 I got a tattoo based on a famous photo of Dan. It's him smiling, handcuffed, flashing a peace sign, taken around when he stood trial for burning Vietnam War draft cards with a group of eight other Catholics. The story of the trial is deeply moving: None of the defendants fought the charges; each stood up and testified about why they felt called by their Catholic faith to do something to stop the killing in Vietnam. The judge had a duty to impose the penalty demanded by the law but openly admitted, too, that the testimonies had been stirring and inspiring. So, while awaiting the guilty verdict from the jury, he joined the defendants and the prosecution in a recitation of the Our Father, requested by Dan.[4]

As I was walking out the door to the tattoo shop, my husband asked me, "You're sure he's not going to be revealed as some kind of abuser, right?" I told him I would be very surprised if he were, since I knew a lot of people who knew him and spoke honestly about him, and none of them had hinted at anything like that. But, as my trust in heroes has waned and my perspective on them has grown more honest, I've come to see this image of Dan's handcuffed hands making a peace sign differently: it's less an homage to Dan himself, and more one to this prophetic action. And the hands, belonging to a real human who sinned like the rest of us and not some imagined perfect person, are a sign that even our ordinary, sinful hands can do good, can be tools of God's will. It gives me hope for myself, for my own hands.

In both rounds of revelations about Vanier, I've struggled with the idea that I had to somehow expunge Vanier's teaching from my own brain, his spirituality of brokenness from my own spirituality. And since his teachings were, essentially, teachings about my own call as a Christian, the idea of weeding them out raised for me the question of what essential parts of me might need to come out with it once I started pulling.[5]

The thing is, I don't think that what influenced me from Vanier was bad. I don't think everything he taught or said or did is necessarily undermined by the evil he did. L'Arche is a good thing. Seeing God reaching out to us through others' brokenness and our own is a good thing. Climbing down the ladder, the way Christ did, is a good thing. Humility is a good thing.

So, no, I don't evangelize about Jean Vanier the way I used to. If the last few years have taught me anything, it's that only Jesus is worth evangelizing for. Like the guy from Alcoholics Anonymous said, he's the only one of my heroes who won't let me down.

I don't keep Vanier's photo up anymore, or pray through his intercession, or keep his books on my bookshelf, or listen to his interviews. When he comes up in conversation, I'm honest, both about my disgust and horror at him, and the impact his teaching had on me. I try to be honest. I try to be humble.

CHAPTER 5

Making $aints

"By the end of this, we're probably going to be approaching a million dollars," George Horton, the local postulator for Dorothy Day's canonization cause, told me.[1] I don't know why I was so surprised: I was a member of the advisory committee for the cause and had been privy to the financial presentations that laid out our budget each year. I knew canonizing saints was an expensive operation. Still, the number—$1 million spent in total, from 2015 to whenever Dorothy would finally be canonized—made my breath catch in my throat.

Later, a monsignor who had worked in what was then called the Congregation for the Causes of Saints, the Vatican's saint-making office, would tell me blithely that a million was not much, considering that talks about making her a saint had begun just after her death in 1980, so the million dollars should be divided over forty years, resulting in a rather small annual budget. He was wrong: Even considering the forty-year timeline, most experts consider the average canonization cause to cost about €500,000 (over $558,000) from start to finish, with only very high profile causes approaching the million-Euro mark.[2] Dorothy's would be on the expensive side—a great irony for a woman who lived voluntarily in poverty.

That it costs anything at all evinces a strange tension that exists in the church between holiness, which Jesus made clear is easier for the poor to achieve (cf. Matthew 19:24), and the necessity for great sums of money to fund apparently objective official declarations of holiness.

◢ ◢ ◢

COVERING THE VATICAN, I get emails a few times a year with updates from the Vatican's saint-making office, now called the Dicastery for the Causes of Saints. In these reports, a pattern is obvious: the vast majority of sainthood causes that are advancing through its four stages (Servant of God, Venerable, Blessed, and Saint) are typically European—usually Italian, but also many French—priests and nuns. Often they are founders of religious orders. A 2016 study by two Harvard University scholars who analyzed all of the saints canonized between 1590 (when the canonization process was formalized) and 2012 (the end of Benedict XVI's papacy) found that 46 percent of those canonized lived in Italy when they died; 34 percent lived elsewhere in Western Europe, 7 percent in Eastern Europe, 7 percent in Latin America, 4 percent in North America, 2.4 percent in Asia, and only 0.7 percent in Africa.[3]

As I volunteered to work on Dorothy Day's canonization cause, I started to understand how this stratification had come about. Making saints, it turns out, takes a lot of human and financial resources. Just to open a canonization cause will cost the diocese or religious order that the potential saint belonged to €50,000 (over $55,800)—an amount paid to the Vatican's saint-making office. The diocese or order then is tasked with the "local phase" of the canonization cause, which involves putting together transcripts of nearly everything the candidate for canonization has written—for Dorothy, a prolific writer and journalist, this amounted to about ten thousand pages of diaries, plus her many columns in the newspaper she founded, *The Catholic Worker,* and other publications she wrote for—along with transcribed interviews with those who knew the candidate or could speak to how his or her example had inspired others to greater faith. These materials all have to be reviewed by canonical experts and printed according to very specific guidelines.

I first joined Dorothy's canonization cause as a volunteer transcriber after Jeff Korgen, a consultant brought on by the Archdiocese of New York to manage Dorothy's canonization cause starting in 2015, appeared at a Friday night meeting at the Catholic Worker asking for people to help.

After a few months as a volunteer transcriber, Jeff thought my talents as a magazine editor might be better put to use editing other volunteers' transcriptions. Even more important than making sure all of the words were perfectly transcribed, Jeff told me, was ensuring that every transcript was formatted for A4 European paper—a fraction of an inch larger than American letter paper—with a 1.25-inch margin on the left and 1-inch margins on the other sides, double-spaced, in Times New Roman 12.

A single mistake in the formatting of the fifty thousand pages of documentation would result in the Vatican office requiring us to reprint the entire thing, at the archdiocese's expense.

Here's the kicker: In 2016, leaked Vatican documents showed that one of the three print shops that the saint-making office recommended was owned by the family of arguably "the top postulator in the world."[4] A postulator is the person who shepherds a canonization cause through its "Roman phase." The postulator in question, Andrea Ambrosi, had handled the canonization causes of Pope John XXIII, John Henry Newman, Emperor Charles I of Habsburg, Mother Théodore Guérin, and Archbishop Fulton Sheen. He was without doubt the most sought-after postulator for American sainthood causes, and when he retired in 2021 after fifty years of saint-making, his daughter Angelica, who had worked with him for seventeen years, took his place. To put it bluntly, the Ambrosi postulators had almost certainly brought their family's print shop a lot of business.

In 2016, as part of Pope Francis's financial crackdown on mismanagement of money at the Vatican, Ambrosi's three accounts in the Vatican Bank were frozen; they contained about €1 million total.[5] Ambrosi wrote a letter arguing against the freezing of his assets and was never tried for any financial crimes. He continued working with the Vatican for five more years. His family's print shop, Nova Res, is to this day the "most commonly used" of the two shops the Dicastery for the Causes of Saints now recommends, two experts confirmed to me.

The strict formatting requirements for printed documents and the requirement that all documents be submitted in print remain in place, despite Pope Francis's landmark exhortation on the environment, "Laudato Si," issued in 2016, and despite the fact that, according to one well-informed source I spoke to, the dicastery's employees do most of their work on tablets.

❧   ❧   ❧

ONCE A SAINTHOOD cause's documentation arrives in Rome, sealed in archival boxes wrapped in ribbon with a wax seal, the diocese or religious order's work of gathering materials is done, but its regular payments to the saint-making office and to its Roman postulator are just beginning. The Vatican office sends a bill just for opening the boxes.

The Roman phase of a canonization process first involves an employee of the Vatican's saint-making office reading through the materials submitted. For the fifty thousand pages of documentation sent with Dorothy Day's cause—which, because of the volume of her writing, was much more than a typical cause would submit—it was estimated to take about a year.

The Vatican sends a second bill when a relator is appointed to oversee the next phase: the writing of an official, red-bound biography, called a *positio.* For about another year, the postulator, working with another person, has to write the *positio,* laying out arguments for and against her canonization. When it's done, the Vatican sends the diocese or order sponsoring the cause another bill. A team of historians and a separate team of theologians review the *positio* for historical relevance and proof of what the Vatican calls "heroic virtue," and then the bishops and cardinals of the saint-making dicastery meet to decide if the cause is worth presenting to the pope to be moved to the next stage: being named "Venerable." When the dicastery makes its decision, it sends a fourth and final bill.

The next step is to wait for miracles to be reported and confirmed by a team of experts. These are almost always medical miracles, because of how well documented a person's condition before and after an apparently miraculous healing tends to be. Of the doctors asked to verify whether a healing was unexplainable, at least one has to be a non-Catholic. Usually, the postulator is consulting with experts during this process and pays them for their time. Once the Vatican recognizes two miracles—or only one, if you're canonizing a martyr—they are cleared to be approved for sainthood, at which point the diocese or religious order foots the bill for an elaborate canonization ceremony, usually in Rome.

Throughout this process, the diocese or religious order sponsoring the cause is paying the postulator, whose job is essentially to nag the Dicastery for the Causes of Saints to keep working on a cause rather than letting it fall by the wayside. Their rates vary widely, and they can have up to thirty cases open at a time, a limit that was only imposed in 2021.

⁂ ⁂ ⁂

THE VATICAN IS no stranger to financial scandals. It is well known that the Vatican Bank has historically been used for money laundering, including for various political groups, and is rumored to have been linked to the Mafia and Masonic groups. The plot of *The Godfather Part III*—in which a scandal involving the Vatican Bank leads to the murder of John Paul I, who was (in real life) only pope for a month—is based on a real banking scandal, though the rumors that John Paul I was murdered have been thoroughly debunked.[6] Another suspicious death linked to the Vatican Bank has been ruled a murder: that of Roberto Calvi, who was nicknamed "God's Banker" for his close business dealings with the Holy See. Calvi was the chairman of another Italian bank that crashed in the early 1980s; his murder remains unsolved.

These days, much of the coverage of Vatican financial scandals is in the context of Pope Francis's crackdown on financial mismanagement in the Vatican. Some of this started under Pope Benedict XVI, who instituted a financial watchdog group within the Holy See and commissioned a report on the Vatican Bank from Moneyval, an international auditor of money laundering. Moneyval said in its 2012 report that the Vatican had made significant progress but needed further reforms; Pope Francis has continued these and expanded them to include checks and balances on spending by Vatican offices, shutting down more than one thousand Vatican Bank accounts that did not meet certain requirements and imposing guidelines on how the Vatican awards contracts (they can't go to Vatican officials' family members anymore—for those wondering, postulators are not Vatican employees, so the Ambrosis' situation is technically legal). Francis appointed one of Italy's top anti-Mafia prosecutors as president of the Vatican's criminal tribunal and removed cardinals' diplomatic immunity, allowing them to be judged by lay experts for the first time.

Maybe because I have closely covered the Vatican only in this era of reform, I find that I am not usually bothered by financial mismanagement in the Vatican. I, of course, share the concerns of Catholics around the world who want to be sure that the money they give to the church is being invested responsibly and spent primarily on charitable works. The Catholic Church is, after all, the largest nongovernmental provider of education and medical services in the world; it is sometimes called the world's largest charity. No Vatican financial scandal, though, has shaken me the way that learning about the corruption and expense involved in saints' causes has.

◊ ◊ ◊

FROM A YOUNG age, Catholics are introduced to a heavenly cast of friends whom they can turn to in times of need. We become close to them: Many Catholic schools have children write reports on a saint and dress up as them for All Saints'

Day; when we're confirmed, we choose another saint by whose name we are called during the sacrament. At my confirmation, it wasn't, "Colleen, I confirm you" but "Francis de Sales, I confirm you." Catholics identify with the saints at a level that is difficult to explain, so much so that even those who no longer practice will send up a "Tony, Tony, look around; there's something lost that needs to be found" to St. Anthony when their keys are missing, or a prayer to St. Jude in the face of a hopeless cause. We're encouraged to imagine that one day we could be counted among the canonized.

There is plenty to make us skeptical, of course: Some canonized saints and people perceived as holy have done horrible things. Some saints, like Christopher and Ursula, likely never existed. And there is even some truth to the Protestant concern that Catholics' devotion to saints can sometimes distract from our relationship with God.

The thing that bothers me most, though, is how money has made the entire canonization operation unequal. Because of the sheer amount of labor and money it takes to complete the local phase of a canonization cause and finance the Roman phase, canonization is simply impossible for most people. Founders of religious orders have members who can provide free or minimally paid labor for their causes; laypeople and even poor dioceses often don't have access to money or that kind of labor, unless a wealthy donor or group of donors steps in. And because the process can go on for decades, causes sometimes fall by the wayside when the sponsors who were working on it do not pass on their work, or if someone in the next generation fails to take it up. I once spoke with a woman whose great-uncle was up for canonization, but she had no idea where the case stood after her grandfather and his siblings died. She had heard nothing from the great-uncle's religious order, although the family continued to send them money for the cause and a Roman postulator was still assigned to it (and presumably being paid).

I should pause here to say that the church considers that everyone who is in heaven is a lowercase-*s* saint, and canonization is just a special stamp of approval, saying this person is definitely in heaven. But canonization helps spread that person's story, and it is a shame that so few laypeople—who make up the majority of the church—have been given this honor and thus had their stories spread far and wide to inspire other laypeople. It is a shame that so many holy people who were poor, or even middle-class, are never recognized due to lack of funds.

In Antigua Guatemala, one lay Franciscan called Hermano Pedro ("Brother Pedro") was venerated for centuries after his death in 1667. In his short life, just forty-one years, Pedro founded homes for poor, indigenous, and homeless people, a hospital and school that were open to all people regardless of race or sex, and the first religious order—the Bethlehemites—born in the Americas. He famously kept the wealthy aware of the plight of the poor by walking through their neighborhoods ringing a bell. Within a year of his death, his supporters began gathering evidence of his holiness for a possible canonization cause that would take 350 years to complete.

People traveled from all over Central America to pray at

his tomb, knocking on it to make sure he would hear their intercessions. Countless miracles were attributed to him, and a chapel full of crutches left behind by those who said they were healed, reminiscent of the piles of crutches at Lourdes, is still visible at Hermano Pedro's church in Antigua today. When I talk with my co-worker, *America* magazine's Vatican correspondent Gerry O'Connell, about the cost of saint-making, his visit to Antigua with John Paul II in 1983 is the first thing that comes to mind. People had clearly regarded this man as a saint for hundreds of years, yet he went unrecognized. His canonization cause, which advanced to the Venerable stage in 1771, languished in Rome for two hundred years until John Paul II beatified him in 1980; part of this delay was due to a lack of funds.

A local source in Antigua, a historian named Ignacio Ochoa, told me in an interview that he thinks Hermano Pedro's cause was only rescued from obscurity under John Paul because of the civil unrest all over Latin America in the 1970s and 1980s.[7] In an effort to rein in liberation theology, which combined Marxist social analysis with Catholic Social Teaching, John Paul sought out a saint who could inspire Latin Americans but who was not critical of the Spanish colonial structure. Hermano Pedro, a Spanish native, was not, and so, Ignacio said, his cause was chosen from among a few who were being considered. John Paul beatified Hermano Pedro at the Vatican in 1980 and returned to Guatemala to canonize him in 2002.

If Ignacio and Gerry's readings of Hermano Pedro's canonization cause are correct, then they tell an unsettling story of a holy man, venerated for centuries, attributed with miracles, who may never have been canonized because his community could not afford it and whose cause was only finally advanced to protect the political and economic status quo.

How many more Hermano Pedros are out there? Holy people, lowercase-*s* saints who will never be recognized for lack of money? And how many saints have been pushed through, well-funded and canonized quickly, before stains on their past that may have been disqualifying come to light? These questions are enough to shake my faith in the entire canonization system—to say, forget all this, I will pray for whoever's intercession I want to ask for, or even skip the saints altogether and talk only to God, and disregard the church's meaningless declarations of sanctity. It makes me want to pull out of a canonization cause I really believe in— that of Dorothy Day, a laywoman who championed the poor and pacifism and who had an abortion, whose extraordinary life mirrors that of people never enshrined among the canonized before—because that million dollars should go toward the poor rather than printing and shipping fifty thousand pages of paper that could have just been emailed.

🌿 🌿 🌿

YET HERE I am, praying to the saints, working on Dorothy's cause. Exactly one thing keeps me here: miracles.

Miracles are the one part of the canonization process that I really have faith in. As longtime Vatican journalist John Thavis once told me, miracles are God's stamp of approval on a canonization cause. We do all the rest—and gum it up with our money and our political motivations—but a cause cannot move forward without confirmed miracles. The requirements for approving them are stringent, rooted in the church's desire to prove it was not adversarial toward science, and until John Paul II's reforms in 1983, every sainthood candidate had to have four confirmed miracles before they were canonized; sometimes, the Vatican required as many as eight. Today, the requirement is two, or only one for a martyr.

Recently, as part of my work on Dorothy's cause, I went through a spreadsheet of some seven hundred "graces and favors," as possible miracles are officially called, that had been reported as having come about through Dorothy's intercession. Some might indeed meet the Vatican's requirements, if we can get them verified by doctors who had firsthand knowledge of the cases, but it has proven difficult. Many of them are about little differences that prayers to Dorothy have made in people's lives—little miracles, in a way, but ones that don't come close to passing Vatican scrutiny as confirmed miracles. As of writing this chapter, it has been two years since the Roman phase began, and the person overseeing possible miracles does not believe we have any promising leads.

Seeing the difficulty of having miracles verified firsthand has lent some credence to the idea that miracles are "God's stamp of approval" on this otherwise very human process. Anything that makes it through all these hoops could only get there by divine intervention—medically documented

healings, verified by science and non-Catholic doctors, passing Vatican canonists' scrutiny, attributed to only one potential saint (a real challenge, as Catholics in dire situations tend
to call on multiple saints for help). When corruption makes
me want to throw the whole process out, miracles are what
keep me believing that there is some truth to the claim that
capital-*S* saints are in heaven praying for us.

The process, of course, needs major reforms. Financial
ones, as I mentioned before, have been happening since
2016, when Pope Francis took aim at the finances of the
Congregation (now Dicastery) for the Causes of Saints and
the Roman postulators who profit from each cause they are
tasked with advancing. He required an external administra-
tor to oversee the bank account associated with each cause,
to keep a record of all expenditures that were unmonitored
and at times abused until 2016, and to require a report on
each cause to be submitted both to the bishop or superior of
the diocese or religious order sponsoring the cause and to
the Congregation for the Causes of Saints.

Still, it is difficult to tell how effectively these measures
have been enforced, or whether they have made a difference. For example, up until the 2016 reforms, a fund was in
place to help advance underfunded sainthood causes. This
Fund for the Causes of the Poor was to receive a contribu-
tion from every postulator for each cause they presented to
the saint-making office. Once a candidate for sainthood was
named Blessed and the expenses for the cause settled,
20 percent of the money left was to go to this fund, according to the internal reports leaked by the journalist Gianluigi

Nuzzi. The reports said, "From the examination of the books relative to the Fund for the Causes of the Poor presented by the Congregation for recent years, it would appear that these obligations have not been fulfilled. In fact, the above-mentioned Fund has grown in a very limited manner." Nuzzi, in his commentary on the report, interprets this to mean that the fund "was not growing," period.

The 2016 reforms imposed by Pope Francis, which were covered in the press as being focused in part on making the canonization process more equitable and accessible to poorer dioceses, established a similar fund, called the Solidarity Fund.[8] In an interview, Dr. Emanuele Spedicato, an expert who has written multiple books on the canonization process, told me that as far as he knows, the new Solidarity Fund is indeed receiving the contributions it is supposed to, and that its funds are being awarded only to "very poor" causes, although he could not name any examples.

It seems obvious that the financial reforms need to go further, to even the playing field more between well-funded and under-funded causes for canonization. As for how this could be achieved, I don't know. As many Vatican employees will tell you, the offices are understaffed and overworked, so reforms that involve more work for the Vatican are unlikely to happen. But I think an analysis within the Dicastery for the Causes of Saints of what the process actually costs and where expenses might be cut would be a good start.

If I might suggest a starting point: for the love of God, let people submit their documentation as PDFs.[9]

CHAPTER 6

From "I" to "We"

My second trip to Rome was, in many ways, just like the first. I was there to report on yet another big-deal global meeting, the Synod on Synodality, and I spent two weeks crisscrossing St. Peter's Square and the grand Via della Conciliazione that leads up to it, always glancing over at the basilica, remembering the first time I saw it and felt nothing. Each time, I clocked my own inner feeling: still neutral, but somehow richer.

Maybe it was that I knew more than I had four and a half years earlier. For one thing, my job had changed: In addition to hosting and producing the weekly Vatican podcast, I was now also editing, soliciting, and writing Vatican coverage full time. I'd gotten a "permanent" (three-year) Vatican press accreditation and was following every update about every papal meeting and statement and joining Vatican press conferences from my home in New Orleans. I'd gotten to know people who worked in the Vatican day in and day out, people who were trying their best, who had made sacrifices to do church work they believed in, others for whom it was just a job, and some who were drawn to the center of power in the church to serve their own egos. I'd met people who supported the pope and those who didn't, people who held a variety of viewpoints on all of the little decisions he made that most people never hear about, people who seemed to have the sort of interior freedom that only comes from a healthy spiritual life, and people who, as far as I could tell, never thought about God at all.

That is to say, I'd gotten to know the Vatican as a place made up of people; a sort of worldwide company with a ton of mismanagement and corruption that also happened to be the largest charity in the world, with an army of diplomats whose main goal is peace, led by a guy whose election is always surrounded by political battles and gossip but who is also, somehow, chosen by the Holy Spirit.

Believing that—believing all of it, despite knowing so much of what goes on—is a hard ask of anyone. It's impossible to be a Catholic these days without experiencing some cognitive dissonance. We wrestle with the teachings and the institutional problems, think them through and rethink them, and pray for some grace to see God working somewhere in all this. Those of us who take up that wrestling willingly are aspiring to what I call a mature faith.

The institutional Catholic Church is starting to see that laypeople are moving into a more mature faith, too: hence the Synod on Synodality that I was in Rome to cover in October 2023 and 2024. Put simply, a synod is—at least in the Roman Catholic usage—a meeting of bishops centered on a certain topic. They were used in the first millennium of Christianity and fell into disuse sometime after the Eastern and Western Churches split in 1054. After bishops had the experience of working together collegially, including with Eastern bishops, at Vatican II, they asked Pope Paul VI to make synods a regular thing. He did, but it was much more limited in scope than what the Vatican II bishops had in mind: synods basically ended up being meetings of bishops where they would discuss and draft papal documents. They were, by all accounts, pretty boring affairs: I've heard numerous stories of bishops falling asleep in the auditorium-style synod hall while other bishops gave droning, and not infrequently off-topic, speeches.

Under Pope Francis, though, synods changed dramatically and quickly. In the first year of his papacy, Francis called for an extraordinary synod—that is, a synod to be held outside the usual synod meeting schedule—on the family. It would be preceded, for the first time, by a worldwide consultation with Catholics at the parish level about the topics to be discussed. Francis later added on a second, larger meeting the year after that included laypeople in the bishops' small-group discussions for the first time.

Francis held other special-topic synods: on young people (2017), on the Amazon region (2019), and, finally, on synodality itself (2021–2024). All were preceded by listening processes with members of the relevant groups, both Catholic and non-Catholic. The listening process for that last synod reached further than any listening effort in human history: starting at the parish and diocesan level in 2021, Catholic churches, groups, and ministries held listening sessions around three themes: Communion, Participation, and

Mission. The key question was about how the church could better live out its evangelizing mission: that is, helping others have an encounter with Christ, mostly through relationships (rather than one-way proselytizing), and how all Catholics could participate in that. How could laypeople step into their role as protagonists of evangelization rather than being passive members of the church who were expected to, as the tired formulation went, "pay, pray, and obey"? Did structures need to change?

That meant regular Catholics would have to show up, help coordinate this global listening process, and bring their own ideas forward. Like at all previous Francis synods, no topic or idea was taboo—but neither would it be a "parliament," as Francis has often said. More complex than a simple process of democratization, this synod would be a four-year exercise in communal discernment. Francis saw it as an effort to implement Vatican II's vision of the church, which made laypeople active and engaged participants. His critics saw it as an effort to railroad through his agenda.

As a person who deeply feels a vocation to be a lay Catholic, I was thrilled when this synod was announced. Not only would it take laypeople's input seriously, I thought, but it might actually help rebuild some of the institution's credibility after the sexual abuse crisis by widely consulting people for their honest thoughts about what needed to change in the church. It would also build credibility by involving people deeply in discernment based on the needs they expressed and, I hoped, could move the church toward a healthier dynamic between its leaders and ordinary people.

At the same time, I predicted it would encounter resistance, and I was proven right almost immediately. A month before the synodal process opened, my colleague Doug Girardot and I undertook a massive reporting project: We contacted every diocese and eparchy (the analogue to a diocese for Eastern Catholics) in America and asked them if they had taken the very first step of the synodal process, appointing a person in the diocese to coordinate their listening efforts. By the time the synod officially opened—a year and a half after it was first announced in March 2020—only half of them had, and many hadn't done much beyond that first step.[1]

Obviously, the coronavirus pandemic threw a wrench in the process. But another part of the problem was that when the listening sessions were announced in April 2021, some of our sources explained, their dioceses had already made the budget for their next financial year. They had had no resources set aside for this unforeseen Vatican project. The Vatican's synod office responded by extending the deadline by a few months, until August 2022. Even with the extension, though, the synod didn't catch on in the United States the way it did elsewhere. Participation was rather low—about 1 percent of Catholics, which is still about 668,000 people—and when it came time for there to be continental meetings where people would read the feedback, discern together what had emerged, and send a report to the Vatican, North America was the only continent that refused to meet in person, despite being arguably the easiest to organize, including only the United States and Canada. (Mexico was grouped with Latin America; Oceania included twenty-one countries.) Anecdotally, when I asked my own pastor about our parish's synod plans, he asked me, "Isn't that just a meeting about how to have meetings?"

I admit that, yes, "a meeting on meetings" is exactly what a "Synod on Synodality" sounds like to anyone who previously had a concept of what a synod was in the Catholic Church, and to those who didn't, it meant nothing at all. The branding was terrible, the pitch complicated, and the logo looked like something that might decorate a kindergarten classroom. The Vatican's synod office knew that communicating about the synod was an uphill battle: their communications manager memorably told me in an interview about a year into the process that he was no longer using the word "synodality" when talking about the synod. "I prefer to talk about a 'listening church' [or] 'walking together,'" he said.

Likewise it was difficult to communicate about the synod because people, especially in the anglophone world, projected both their hopes and their fears onto the process. Some progressives hoped and conservatives feared that the synod would bring married priests, women deacons, maybe even women priests; other progressives feared that after all this listening, nothing at all would change. Many conservative American Catholics seemed content to let it pass by; many others likely never heard about it. Some, like outspoken American Francis-critic Cardinal Raymond Burke, did all they could to discredit the process: Burke wrote the preface to a book that compared the synodal process to a "Pandora's box" that would unleash havoc in the church; on the eve of the synod's first global meeting in Rome, he spoke at a conference called "The Synodal Babel," comparing it to the biblical story of the Tower of Babel—a human effort to overcome the need for God, which resulted in the disintegration of the community.

Still, in my reporting, I encountered plenty of people from around the world who were taking the synodal process seriously, even passionately. One nun in Chad explained to me how she organized a listening session with the children in her parish—many of them orphans—who surprised her by saying that they wanted their elders to stop shielding them from funerals. They said they wanted to be part of all of the church's services. Another nun, in the United States, had been appointed to lead the synod process for one of the dioceses that had a robust synod listening program. She'd experienced communal discernment in her religious order for decades and was thrilled to teach it to other Catholics and see what emerged. A laywoman in Atlanta even printed a giant decal of Pope Francis for the back of her car that said, "Pope Francis wants to hear from you!" and included her email. She held listening sessions with anyone who wanted to talk with her, including homeless, incarcerated, and queer people, and sent some six hundred pages to the Vatican's synod office, which welcomed feedback from outside the parish and diocese structure. The Vatican even reached out to Catholic social-service organizations that served people who might have been overlooked—migrants, prisoners, and so on—to make sure they were casting a wide net.[2]

All of this feedback was synthesized first at the diocesan level, then the regional level (at least in the United States), then the level of the bishops' conference. These reports, along with those from outside the diocese structure, went to a group of experts in synodality who gathered in Frascati, Italy, to put together a guiding document for continental discernment meetings. Reports from those meetings went back to the Vatican's synod office, and they formed the basis for the document that would guide the first of two synod assemblies in the Vatican gathering representatives from around the world for a month to discuss and discern together what was emerging.

The Rome meetings were going to be a huge deal. For the first time, a meeting of the synod of bishops was going to include laypeople as full voting members—including 54 women out of the 365 participants. Remember how there had been the controversy for years over lay brothers being able to vote, but not women? Most participants at the synod were still bishops, but the involvement of women was nonetheless unwelcome by some: one prelate, in the second week of the synod, stormed out of the meeting, saying, "This is not a synod of bishops!"

I traveled to Rome for two weeks to cover that meeting in October 2023. Vatican reporting is often challenging because few people are ever willing to speak on the record, and this meeting was no exception: at the very beginning, Pope Francis asked the synod members to "fast" from speaking to the media and to keep their own "interventions" (Vaticanese for speeches) and those of others private. Though the

Vatican's press office offered media briefings almost every day, the information they released was sparse. A Vatican spokesman told us repeatedly that conversations in the synod were "serene"; meanwhile, we reporters were hearing off the record about tense moments like the one I just described, when the prelate stormed out. There was a sense that everyone was waiting for the "Pachamama" of this synod—referring to when, during the Amazon synod, some opponents of the gathering spotted two indigenous statues of naked pregnant women at a prayer service in the Vatican gardens and declared that the Vatican was promoting worship of the Andean goddess Pachamama (which the statues did not resemble). A publicity stunt followed in which a young man stole the statues and threw them into the Tiber River. Video of the incident was edited by U.S. Francis-critic YouTuber Taylor Marshall and distributed on traditionalist websites; the Roman police eventually recovered the statues and returned them; the pope and a member of the press corps apologized to the indigenous synod representatives; the statue thief was hailed as a hero and went on a speaking tour around the United States.

Thankfully, no Pachamama moment came in this synod. Chatting with me in St. Peter's Square one morning three weeks into the synod, one of the most prominent cardinals in the meeting told me he was pleasantly surprised with how well the journalists were behaving.

Despite the hope I had in the synod project, the day-to-day of covering it felt less hopeful. Producing podcasts and articles every day, trying to get quotes from synod members as they walked into or left the synod hall, and sprinting home after off-record dinners to jot down everything I could remember from the conversation was exhausting. Like during my first visit to Rome, I barely had time or energy to stop into a church or offer up a quick prayer. I was sure the Holy Spirit was working in the synod hall—in me, not so much.

A couple of days into my work there, my grandfather, who had recently moved into a nursing home, went into hospice and died soon after. Far from home, I oscillated between numbness and grief, wanting solitude and seeking out others. I distracted myself with my work as much as possible and mentioned my grandfather's passing to almost no one.

One person who did know was our permanent Vatican correspondent, Gerry. I have been good friends with Gerry since we started our weekly Vatican podcast years ago; now he is someone I know I can call for life advice or a chat at any time. Days after the synod opened, Gerry's wife, renowned war correspondent Elisabetta Piqué, was sent to Israel to cover the horrifying violence that was unfolding after Hamas's attack on Israel on October 7. She was there the whole month; sometimes I would sit with Gerry in his living room and watch Betta's TV broadcasts—her in one window, a panoramic shot of the Gaza City skyline on the other that was waiting to catch any explosions happening in real time.

One night, before going to dinner at Gerry's, I stopped into the church of Sant'Andrea della Valle for an evening Mass. I had mostly wanted to go there because I love the opera *Tosca* that is set there and wanted to see it in person; when I arrived, though, I realized it was the first moment I'd had to pray since my grandpa's death.

The Mass was immensely comforting: I thought I would be alone, but just as it was about to start, my co-worker Ashley arrived and sat next to me. The priest was droning, the congregation was ancient, the choir was wavering, but all of this unexpectedly comforted me: it was, despite being thousands of miles away, just like home.

Afterward, at Gerry's, I was grateful to just sit in the presence of others, knowing we each knew what the others were struggling with, knowing we were in it together.

At a retreat for synod members just before the Roman meeting started, one of the synod's two spiritual guides, Fr. Timothy Radcliffe, OP, told the participants that their job over the next days and weeks would be to "move from 'I' to 'we.'"

"The foundation of everything that we are going to do in the next three weeks should be the friendships we create with each other," Radcliffe said. "It does not look [like] much. It will not make headlines in the media. 'They came all the way to Rome to make friendships! What a waste!' But it is by friendship that we shall make the transition, as [synod spiritual guide] Madre Maria Grazia [Angelini, OSB] said, from 'I' to 'We.'"

One way they would do this was through a unique method called "Conversation in the Spirit," derived from a Canadian Jesuit method for group discernment. The synod members practiced it at the retreat, and it was how all of the

deliberations in the synod hall were structured. Having re-
flected and prayed with the question they'd be discussing,
which was based on the feedback from the global listening
sessions, the small-group members would sit together at a
round table of about ten people. They would introduce
themselves with the name they would like to go by (some
bishops opted for their first names, others "Bishop So-
and-So"); there would be an opening prayer, and then each
person would offer a three-minute reflection on what had
emerged in their prayer. No one was allowed to interrupt,
and they were not to respond to what others had said until
the next round. There would be a few minutes for silent
prayer, then the group would go around again, responding
to what they had heard. This wasn't a chance to argue but
rather to name what spoke to them or made them uncom-
fortable, or to identify common threads or tensions among
what everyone had said. Then more prayer. By the third
round, some key ideas would emerge. The group discussed
those and wrote a brief two-page report on the convergen-
ces, divergences, remaining questions, and proposals that
came out of their conversation.

I was surprised to hear, over and over from synod members, that these conversations were proving transformative.
Of course, some participants told me that certain members
had used "round two to continue their speech from round
one" rather than listening to others, and I heard that a frequent refrain from facilitators was "She hasn't quite finished, Your Eminence," implying it took some time for even
the cardinals in the room to stop interrupting the women.

But by and large, the people I spoke to really felt that the conversation method was giving them a sense of the Holy Spirit at work through their fellow synod members, even those with whom they disagreed.

One synod member, Fr. Vimal Tirimanna, a funny and outspoken theologian from Sri Lanka, told me, "[At] first, I thought it was pious nonsense to 'talk in the spirit,' spiritual conversation. I said, 'This is going to be a blessed headache!'

"Now, these round tables challenged me a lot," he continued. "It became a discipline, dear Colleen, in my life. I'm trying now, even in my classes here, in my lectures, in my way of doing things, I'm trying my best to follow that method, to listen."

I shouldn't have been surprised to hear this. After all, one of the key ideas Pope Francis has returned to repeatedly in my time reporting on his speeches and documents has been the transformative power of personal encounters and conversations, especially with those who are different from you. It was something I'd experienced a million times myself, sitting late into the night or passing a slow afternoon at the Catholic Worker, sitting on strangers' front porches in New Orleans, talking with friends or family whose life experiences and beliefs were different from my own. Meeting people in person, giving them your undivided attention, really listening and sharing and finding common ground— these are essential parts of dialogue and of the human experience, and they're things that many of us experienced a lot less of during the pandemic. The effects of that isolation have lingered and festered.

A few weeks into the synod, Fr. Radcliffe surprised us reporters by confirming, in one of his public addresses, a story that many synod members had shared as one of the most impactful moments of the meeting: After a day of contentious conversations about how exactly the church should balance what the synod framed as the tension between love and truth when ministering to LGBT Catholics, a young woman, one of the youngest participants, stood up to give the last intervention of the day. She used her time—speaking with great courage, by all accounts, to a crowd of mostly bishops—to tell them about her sister, who was bisexual and had been denied absolution when she went to confession. The sister had died by suicide.

You could hear a pin drop, synod participants told me. Some were so overwhelmed with emotion that they left the room. "Many of us wept when we heard of that young woman who committed suicide because she was bisexual and did not feel welcomed in the church," Radcliffe said to the synod hall. I was up high, in the press box. "I wept," he continued. "I hope it changed us."

A FEW DAYS BEFORE I left Rome was an important feast day for the Religious of the Sacred Heart, the order of nuns who had educated me from age four to fourteen back in St. Charles, Missouri. One of the sisters I'd served on a committee with, Mary, who was living in Rome and whom I'd only ever met on Zoom, invited me to come celebrate the feast day with her community.

She showed me around the villa that serves as the order's

headquarters, and I was struck by how familiar it all felt: The religious images and symbols, of course, were the same ones the order displayed at the school I'd attended, but even the feel of the place was the same. The building was full of big, sunny windows; there were lots of little nooks for conversation here and there, each with at least two comfortable chairs; the design of the renovated villa was the same tasteful mix of traditional and modern that my old nineteenth-century French-style school building, with expansions cobbled on over the decades, had been.

After our tour and dinner with the community, Mary and I fell onto one of the couches in the dining room, me with a glass of wine. We sat there like schoolgirls—her feet up on the table, mine tucked under me, sitting sideways, resting my wineglass on the couch back—and soon she was telling me about one of her dearest friends, another nun in her order, who had had cancer. She described how, unexpectedly, they'd ended up spending her friend's last Christmas together (the subtext of course being that it was divine providence, though to say that would have been to destroy the silent understanding we shared). She told me about her friend's last days, how her friend had kept her sense of humor even as her body wasted away, how her death was surprisingly beautiful—exactly how my mom had described my grandpa's passing to me a few days before. We cried together, and laughed, and felt at peace.

When I look back on the synod, I realize that the people inside the synod and the friends I spent time with outside the synod were on parallel journeys: from isolation and loneliness (at least on my part; I spend much of my time alone, much more than I would like) to encounter, transformation, and community.

THE 2023 SYNOD meeting's final days were frantic. The schedule changed every twelve hours, with last-minute notifications going out that the drafting committee needed more time to prepare the synthesis report. Its first draft garnered one thousand proposed amendments. Fr. Vimal told me that the fact that the document had come together at all before the meeting concluded was "a miracle."

Part of the "miracle" may have been that the drafters skipped over things that risked not meeting the two-thirds majority required for each paragraph to pass. The biggest omission: LGBT issues, which we know were discussed at length, were not mentioned at all in the document, not even after the stunning speech the young woman had given about her sister. There was one brief mention in the document of "matters of identity and sexuality" needing further discernment, but that was it. Likewise, the "divergences" that had been reported by the small groups had been reworked—when Gerry asked at a Vatican press conference where the divergences had gone, a spokesperson responded that they'd been incorporated into the sections on questions for further discernment.

Still, some decisive things did come out in the document: The Roman assembly, like the continental, regional, and local gatherings before it, overwhelmingly said that women needed to be involved in church leadership and decision-making "urgently." They called for the secret reports from two previous Vatican commissions that had studied women deacons to be submitted to their assembly the next year. They called for women to be allowed to be judges in canonical (church law) processes and for a commission to be formed to study what changes in canon law might be needed to give women more authority.

Likewise they focused on an urgent need for formation in synodality. You can't expect a church used to a "command and control" structure, as Pope Francis biographer Austen Ivereigh calls it, to pivot to a model of cooperation and shared responsibility without some serious education and practice. They called for spaces for synodal discussions to be set up in every diocese and for "conversations in the Spirit" to happen around diocesan decisions. They also asked that, between the 2023 and 2024 meetings, there be a global consultation with people in charge of seminary formation, to discuss how priests might be better trained in synodal leadership and service.

I can't say what will happen in the 2024 meeting, or even after that. It's been clear from the beginning that Pope Francis sees this as just one step, our first round of practicing synodality on this scale, that he hopes will be the first of many. Much of that depends on future leaders. Already, it seems to me, there is pushback from some of the bishops who were part of the synod: although only one stormed out saying, "This is not a synod of bishops," several, even those who are very supportive of the synodal project, have voiced that there may need to be a bishops-only synod after any of these "ecclesial assemblies" (assemblies that include bishops, priests, and laypeople) so that the bishops can make decisions together on their own. There's also been concern that the synod will not be able to take on controversial issues at the 2024 meeting because many of those have been assigned to separate "study groups" outside the synod. We'll have to see what happens.

My inward tendency is still toward hope: not for any specific reforms, per se, but hope that the church is starting to do what Pope John XXIII said it needed to do with Vatican II: "open the windows of the Church so that we can see out and the people can see in." Pope Francis echoed this in his pre-conclave speech, the one many say is the reason he was elected pope: "The Church is called to come out of herself and to go to the peripheries. . . . In Revelation, Jesus says that he is at the door and knocks [Revelation 3:20]. Obviously, the text refers to his knocking from the outside in order to enter, but I think about the times in which Jesus knocks from within so that we will let him come out."

The synod process really does feel like the Spirit is moving in the church. It feels like something big and historic is happening. It gives me hope that maybe, by listening to the people in the pews, the institution can grow and heal from the abuse crisis and from its crisis of credibility. It gives me hope that Catholic laypeople are being taken seriously by the hierarchy and are growing into a more mature faith, taking greater responsibility in a church that badly needs us to.

So much of what's recounted in this book, so many of the struggles I've had with Catholicism in the last several years, I've felt I was undertaking alone. Yet over and over again in conversations, I found other people were struggling with the same thing: the same disillusionment, the same destroyed trust, the same disgust at the continually unfolding headlines, and also feeling that they were wrestling alone with what role Catholicism or the Catholic Church should play in their lives. People find different answers: seek out a parish of like-minded people, take some time away from going to Mass, keep going out of willpower or stubbornness or habit or devotion or because they don't know who they are without it. In those moments of conversation, though, we learn we aren't alone. For just a second, there's someone who understands our struggle. I've been lucky, at different times, to work and wrestle and pray alongside people who are going through the same thing, who have the same front-row view I do into the nastiness of the church. It helps to have that community of strugglers.

I think part of why the synod gives me so much hope is that it was an experience of strugglers coming together, seeing one another's difficulties with the church, voicing the difficulties that had surfaced in similar conversations in their home contexts, and not dismissing them but taking them seriously. Saying, "I recognize your struggle. I know it, too, in my own way." Bishops saying it to laypeople. Laypeople saying it back to bishops.

I've talked about the synod as a maturing in faith. But I think the spiritual insight I gained from my few moments of consolation during the 2023 synod was that that maturing can't happen—at least not to its fullest extent—without cooperation. Laypeople can't take on greater roles of responsibility if the bishops don't allow it. Bishops will continue to be lonely and overworked if they don't invite others to share the work. The maturing doesn't happen alone: It happens together. It happens in "Conversations in the Spirit" with capital letters and in regular conversations, where the spirit can move, too. It happens grieving with a nun you just met. It happens sitting in silent companionship, watching your friend's wife on TV, when you're suddenly stirred to pray for her, and you're sure your friend is, too. Maturing in faith happens when Jacob is wrestling with the angel, when Mary Magdalene is proclaiming the Resurrection, when I'm telling Simon he was right about Latin Mass, when someone is emailing me to "keep the faith" after the Vanier revelations, when we're sitting around at the Catholic Worker sharing our hesitations and hopes about Dorothy's canonization.

Dorothy famously wrote at the end of her autobiography, *The Long Loneliness,* that "the final word is love," that "our very faith in love has been tried through fire.

"We cannot love God unless we love each other, and to love we must know each other," she continues. We must share ourselves with others, let them share themselves with us, and love them as we struggle along. And in that, we learn to love Jesus, who shares our struggle more intimately than we can understand. She concludes:

We know him in the breaking of bread, and we are not alone anymore. Heaven is a banquet and life is a banquet, too, even with a crust, where there is companionship.

We have all known the long loneliness and we have learned that the only solution is love and that love comes with community.

It all happened while we sat there talking, and it is still going on.

Afterword

I began writing this book when I was pregnant with my first child, William, and am completing it when he is one and a half, an absolute wonder of running and babbling and playing with toy fire trucks, which he calls "wee-woos."

Writing the book while becoming a parent has both deepened my relationship with God and, at the same time, ratcheted up the stakes of my grappling with the institutional church, especially as I had William baptized into it.

I think it has given me some insights that are sorely missing from most church leaders. They cannot understand, the way I do, the fear that comes from introducing one's own child into an institution infamous for its abuse of children. Yes, I know the data says that abuse is no more common in the church than outside of it, but the concern and lack of trust are more difficult to shake than people know.

At the same time, I've been transformed by the experience of watching my child sleep, feeling such deep love for him, and realizing that that is how God looks at each of us. I've felt intense and ongoing pain, not just in delivering my child but in feeding him from my own body, an exhausting and difficult feat, despite how beautiful and peaceful it appears. Because of this I know, in a way no Catholic priest does, what it means to say, "This is my body, broken and given for your sake."

In a similar way, I know that I cannot understand certain aspects of others' insights into God. I don't know what it's like to give up having a family in order to serve one's religious community. I don't have years of theological study behind me, or the experience of trying to run a parish.

What I do know, though, is that each of our perspectives will only ever be partial understandings of God and of how to make the institutional church more of a spiritual home than a spiritual hurdle. As I wrote in the introduction, our honest conversations and solidarity with one another are the path to healing.

As of this writing, the 2024 synod meeting has concluded, carrying forward many of the themes of the 2023 meeting and codifying them into concrete recommendations, which Pope Francis then adopted as his own official teaching.

Parish councils—one of the most common ways laypeople are involved in parish governance—have been made mandatory and are required to make public reports each year on their work and their membership. Bishops, if they choose to carry out a synodal consultation and then make a decision counter to that consultation's recommendations, have to explain publicly why they chose a different route. And, to our astonishment, the synod's final document said specifically that the question of ordaining women to the diaconate "remains open. This discernment needs to continue." Elsewhere in the same paragraph—the one that received the most "no" votes, though it still passed by a good margin—the synod body wrote, "There is no reason or impediment that should prevent women from carrying out leadership roles in the Church: what comes from the Holy Spirit cannot be stopped."[1]

A few loose ends from the synod remain to be wrapped up: The study groups on controversial issues, like women's ministries, have yet to turn in their work, nor has the canon law commission recommended legal changes for implementing synodality.

Still, as people constantly said during the synod, "The toothpaste is out of the tube." There is no going back. The final document included checklists for implementation, and Pope Francis told bishops they were required to report on their progress at their *ad limina* visits to Rome every few years. I cannot say with certainty what will come from all this, but my hope is that it is only the beginning of our church's transformation into one that welcomes and hears the voices of all baptized people, even those who struggle with the institution or feel they no longer have a place in it. All of these experiences should be part of our understanding of the church's reality—after all, the church is the whole People of God—and we need to be honest about that reality in order to move forward, to earn credibility, to heal.

In the meantime, I will do my best to continue revealing that truth in my work. And at home, I will teach my one-year-old the fundamental truth that he can understand: that God loves him, and all of us, infinitely; that we all have a place at his table.

Acknowledgments

Thanks first of all to my husband, Simon, who has always been willing to do anything that would help me achieve my dreams, including that of writing a book. I love you, and I am grateful every day for you and William. Thank you for happily taking on the added challenge of supporting me through book writing the same year we became parents! This book would have been impossible without you.

Thanks to my editor, Matt Burdette, who dreamed up this idea with me and whose patient and insightful editing and encouragement helped make this book something to be proud of. Thank you to the team at Image Books for believing this book could make a difference for people, and for working so hard to get it into their hands.

I was lucky to work with the great literary agent Roger Freet on this project before his untimely death from pancreatic cancer. Roger, thank you for caring so much. Thank you, too, to Claudia Cross at Folio, who so graciously stepped in as my agent during a time of grief.

My *America* colleagues and mentors were endlessly supportive through this process. Special thanks to James Martin, SJ, and James T. Keane, who first told me I could write a book and who helped me learn how, and to Gerard O'Connell, my mentor in all things Vatican.

A journalist is nothing without her sources. Thank you all, sincerely, for trusting me.

Finally, to the countless friends and family members who have helped me grow in faith and love. Mom and Dad, Claire, Cat, Stephen and Emilia, Vivian, Anna, Alyssa, Mark, Ellie, Chase, Anitta, both the Sams, and our Christina—thank you for being the community that has taught me unconditional love by example for my entire life. Believing in a God who loves unconditionally is easy having loved and been loved by all of you.

Notes

Introduction

1. David Gibson, *The Rule of Benedict: Pope Benedict XVI and His Battle with the Modern World* (HarperCollins, 2007) 374. Kindle edition.

Chapter 1

1. Really, the abuse coverage had amped up in January 2018, when Pope Francis visited Chile and infamously accused three abuse survivors of "calumny." After significant criticism, the pope sent abuse investigator Archbishop Charles Scicluna to Chile. Scicluna turned in a report in April of that year proving the survivors correct, and in May, Pope Francis ordered every bishop in Chile to submit their resignations. He had only accepted seven as of March 9, 2023, according to a report by Loup Besmond de Senneville in *La Croix International.*
2. Vatican Radio, "Holy See Press Office Issues Statement on Pope's Meeting with Kim Davis," News.va, October 2, 2015, https://web.archive.org/web/20151103063802/http://www.news.va/en/news/holy-see-press-office-issues-statement-on-popes-me.
3. These were the National Catholic Register and LifeSite News in the United States, La Verità in Italy, and InfoVaticana in Spain, all of which had been highly critical of Pope Francis.
4. Sixteenth Sunday in Ordinary Time (United States Conference of Catholic Bishops, 2011), https://bible.usccb.org/bible/readings/072124.cfm.

5. *The New American Bible Revised Edition* (Confraternity of Christian Doctrine, 2010) will be referenced throughout this book.
6. Sharon Otterman, "Man Says Cardinal McCarrick, His 'Uncle Ted,' Sexually Abused Him for Years," *New York Times,* July 19, 2018, https://www.nytimes.com/2018/07/19/nyregion /mccarrick-cardinal-sexual-abuse.html.
7. Karen J. Terry et al., *The Causes and Context of Sexual Abuse of Minors by Catholic Priests in the United States, 1950–2010* (United States Conference of Catholic Bishops, 2011; repr.).
8. "Briefing 2019-02-21," YouTube, February 21, 2019, https:// www.youtube.com/watch?v=GeJwGQebF48.
9. "Meeting on 'The Protection of Minors in the Church'— Reflection Points, 21.02.2019," Holy See Press Office, February 21, 2019, https://press.vatican.va/content/salastampa/en /bollettino/pubblico/2019/02/21/190221f.html.

Chapter 2

1. Nathan Schneider, "The Choreography in Rome," *America Media,* June 6, 2015, https://www.americamagazine.org/content /all-things/choreography-rome.
2. This report has since been removed from *L'Osservatore Romano*'s website, but an article on it from *The New York Times* can be found archived here: https://www.nytimes.com/2018/03/01/world /europe/vatican-catholic-church-nuns-work.html.
3. Benedicte Lutaud's excellent book, *Femmes des Papes,* provides a helpful timeline of these reports in its introduction and in its chapter on Lucetta Scaraffia.
4. Like the other reports Ms. Scaraffia's staff published, this article is no longer available online. A report on it from the Associated Press can be found here: https://www.americamagazine .org/politics-society/2019/02/01/vatican-magazine-denounces -sexual-abuse-nuns-priests.
5. Lucetta and I spoke in French together, our only common language at the time. The translations provided are my own.
6. Nicole Winfield, "Pope Publicly Acknowledges Clergy Sexual

Abuse of Nuns," Associated Press, February 5, 2019, https://
apnews.com/article/397f2c76afc04532908035a66ccaacc8.

7. Lila Rice Goldenberg, "#NunsToo: How the Catholic Church
Has Worked to Silence Women Challenging Abuse," *Washington
Post,* April 17, 2019, https://www.washingtonpost.com/out
look/2019/04/17/nunstoo-how-catholic-church-has-worked
-silence-women-challenging-abuse/.

8. Colleen Dulle, "Women Are Rising to New Heights at the Vatican. Could They Change the Church Forever?," *America* magazine, September 16, 2021, https://www.americamagazine.org
/faith/2021/09/16/vatican-top-women-change-smerilli-becquart
-scaraffia-241413.

9. María Lía Zervino, "Dear Pope Francis: Thank You for 8 Years
of Challenging and Healing the Church. But Women Still Deserve More," *America* magazine, March 12, 2021, https://www
.americamagazine.org/faith/2021/03/12/open-letter-pope-francis
-anniversary-catholic-women-240218.

10. Lucetta Scaraffia, interview with Colleen Dulle, *Inside the Vatican,* podcast audio, March 21, 2019, https://www.americamag
azine.org/faith/2019/03/21/how-things-are-changing-women
-vatican-233486.

11. Valentina Alazraki. Used with author's permission.

12. Philip Pullella, "A Popular Pope, but How Powerful? Francis Still
Fights Internal Battles," Reuters, June 27, 2018, https://www
.reuters.com/article/uk-pope-reform-insight-idUKKBN1JN266/.

13. See John L. Allen's June 7, 2022, analysis in *Crux:* https://
cruxnow.com/news-analysis/2022/06/new-hr-office-could-be
-real-revolution-at-heart-of-popes-reform.

14. John L. Allen Jr., "Workers (Again, and Again) Beg the Vatican
to Face Its Personnel Problem," *Crux,* July 14, 2024, https://
cruxnow.com/news-analysis/2024/07/workers-again-and-again
-beg-the-vatican-to-face-its-personnel-problem.

Chapter 3

1. Congregation for the Clergy, "The Gift of the Priestly Vocation:
Ratio Fundamentalis Institutionis Sacerdotalis," Dicastero Per

Il Clero, January 3, 2017, https://www.clerus.va/content/dam
/clerus/documenti/ratio-2026/Ratio-EN-2017-01-03.pdf.

2. Pope Francis, "Post-Synodal Apostolic Exhortation *Amoris Laetitia,*" Vatican.va, March 19, 2016, https://www.vatican.va
/content/dam/francesco/pdf/apost_exhortations/documents/papa
-francesco_esortazione-ap_20160319_amoris-laetitia_en.pdf.

3. Cindy Wooden, "Annulment Process to Be Less Costly, with
'Correct Simplicity,'" Catholic News Service/*America* magazine, September 8, 2015, https://www.americamagazine.org
/issue/annulment-process-be-less-costly-correct-simplicity.

4. Francis, "*Amoris Laetitia,*" footnote 351.

5. Edward Pentin, "Full Text and Explanatory Notes of Cardinals'
Questions on 'Amoris Laetitia,'" *National Catholic Register,*
November 14, 2016, https://www.ncregister.com/blog/full
-text-and-explanatory-notes-of-cardinals-questions-on-amoris
-laetitia.

6. "Correctio Filialis de Haeresibus Propagatis," Correctiofilialis
.org, July 16, 2017, https://www.correctiofilialis.org/.

7. Carlo Maria Viganò and Robert Moynihan, "Letter #32, Friday,
October 30, 2020: Viganò to Trump," *Inside the Vatican,* October 30, 2020, https://insidethevatican.com/news/newsflash
/letter-32-friday-october-30-2020-vigano-to-trump/.

8. Pope Francis, "Traditionis Custodes," Vatican.va, July 16, 2021,
https://www.vatican.va/content/francesco/en/motu_proprio
/documents/20210716-motu-proprio-traditionis-custodes.html.

9. Pope Francis, "Letter of the Holy Father Francis to the Bishops
of the Whole World, That Accompanies the Apostolic Letter
Motu Proprio Data 'Traditionis Custodes,'" Vatican.va, July 16,
2021, https://www.vatican.va/content/francesco/en/letters/2021
/documents/20210716-lettera-vescovi-liturgia.html.

10. For a well-researched and accessible account of how and why
this shift happened, see Mark S. Massa, SJ, *The American Catholic Revolution: How the Sixties Changed the Church Forever* (Ox-
ford University Press, 2010).

11. Colleen Dulle, Jonathan Culbreath, personal, August 19, 2021.

12. Jonathan Culbreath, "I Love Latin Mass and Pope Francis.
Please Don't Let a Few (Very Loud) Traditionalists Ruin It for

the Rest of Us," *America* magazine, July 27, 2021, https://www
.americamagazine.org/faith/2021/07/27/pope-francis-latin
-mass-traditionis-custodes-241121.
13. Gerard O'Connell, "Pope Francis on Plane: 'I Am Not Afraid of
Schisms. I Pray They Do Not Happen,'" *America* magazine, September 10, 2019, https://www.americamagazine.org/faith/2019
/09/10/pope-francis-plane-i-am-not-afraid-schisms-i-pray-they
-do-not-happen.

Chapter 4

1. Bernard Granger et al., "Control and Abuse Investigation on
Thomas Philippe, Jean Vanier and L'Arche (1950–2019),"
Study Commission Mandated by L'Arche International, January 30, 2023, https://commissiondetude-jeanvanier.org/com
missiondetudeindependante2023-empriseetabus/wp-content
/uploads/2023/01/Report_Control-and-Abuse_EN.pdf, 560.
2. Colleen Dulle, "How Can I Reconcile the Good and Evil of
Jean Vanier?," *America* magazine, February 22, 2020, https://
www.americamagazine.org/faith/2020/02/22/how-can
-reconcile-good-evil-jean-vanier.
3. Granger et al., "Control and Abuse Investigation," 832–33.
4. Jim Forest, *At Play in the Lions' Den: A Biography and Memoir of
Daniel Berrigan* (Orbis Books, 2017), 133–34.
5. Jenna Barnett grappled in greater depth with this question in an
exceptional podcast series called *Lead Us Not,* produced by *So-
journers* magazine, which features interviews with L'Arche
members and some of Vanier's victims.

Chapter 5

1. Colleen Dulle and George Horton, Dorothy Day Canonization
Cause, personal, December 2, 2021.
2. Arun Rath and John L. Allen, "Catholic Church Examines Financial Cost of Sainthood, Other," *All Things Considered* (NPR,

February 23, 2014), and Gerard O'Connell, "Pope Francis Brings New Transparency to the Cost of Making Saints," *America* magazine, March 23, 2016, https://www.americamagazine .org/issue/money-and-saint-making.

3. Robert J. Barro and Rachel M. McCleary, "Saints Marching In, 1590–2012," *Economica* 83, no. 331 (June 2016): 385–415, https://doi.org/10.1111/ecca.12196.

4. Gianluigi Nuzzi, *Merchants in the Temple: Inside Pope Francis's Secret Battle Against Corruption in the Vatican* (Henry Holt and Company, 2015). Kindle edition.

5. Nuzzi, *Merchants in the Temple.*

6. See Stefania Falasca's *The September Pope: The Final Days of John Paul I* (Our Sunday Visitor, 2021), considered the decisive work on the subject.

7. Interviewed February 1, 2024. Thanks to Elizabeth Bell in Antigua for setting up the interview.

8. O'Connell, "Pope Francis Brings New Transparency to the Cost of Making Saints."

9. This chapter would not have been possible without lengthy interviews with Msgr. Robert Sarno, a retired official of the Dicastery for the Causes of Saints, and Ken Woodward, author of *Making Saints: How the Catholic Church Determines Who Becomes a Saint, Who Doesn't, and Why* (Touchstone, 1996), for a deep dive episode of my podcast *Inside the Vatican.* The episode elaborates much more than this chapter does on the historic evolution of the canonization process and potential reforms to it. Listen at: https://www.americamagazine.org/faith/2023/02 /16/how-saints-are-made-244753.

Chapter 6

1. Colleen Dulle and Doug Girardot, "We Contacted Every Diocese in the U.S. About Their Synod Plans. Here's What We Found," *America* magazine, October 18, 2021, https://www .americamagazine.org/faith/2021/10/18/synod-bishops-us -diocese-plan-241671.

2. Colleen Dulle, "Deep Dive: The 'Synod on Synodality'—
What's Done and What Comes Next?," *America* magazine, October 14, 2022, https://www.americamagazine.org/faith/2022
/10/14/synodality-walking-together-pope-francis-243970.

Afterword

1. Francis and XVI Ordinary General Assembly of the Synod of
Bishops, "For a Synodal Church: Communion, Participation,
Mission. Final Document," General Secretariat of the Synod,
October 26, 2024, https://www.synod.va/content/dam/synod
/news/2024-10-26_final-document/ENG—Documento-finale
.pdf.

About the Author

COLLEEN DULLE is a multimedia journalist covering Catholic and Vatican news.

As associate editor at America Media, Colleen writes and edits Vatican news and analysis pieces, and hosts and produces the weekly news podcast *Inside the Vatican*. She has commented on Catholic news for a variety of national and international media outlets including the BBC, CBC Radio, and MSNBC.

She is a contributor to Sacred Heart University's *Go, Rebuild My House* church reform blog and serves on the boards of the Ignatian Solidarity Network, the Dorothy Day Guild, and the Visitation Academy of St. Louis.

Colleen's work has earned regional and national accolades from the Catholic Media Association, the Society of Professional Journalists, and the Louisiana-Mississippi Associated Press Media Editors. She was the 2019 and 2021 Catholic Media Association Multimedia Journalist of the Year.

She lives in New Orleans with her husband, Simon; son, William; and dog, Vinny.